FROM SIN *to* SANCTITY

FROM SIN *to* SANCTITY

The Prayers and Meditations of St. Anselm

SAINT ANSELM
of CANTERBURY

TAN Books
Gastonia, North Carolina

Cover design by Jordan Avery
Cover image: *Crucifix with the Magdalene* by Francesco Hayez (1791–1882). Available in the Public Domain (US) / Wikimedia Commons.

Library of Congress Control Number: 2025931185
ISBN: 978-1-5051-3526-8
Kindle ISBN: 978-1-5051-3609-8
ePUB ISBN: 978-1-5051-3608-1

Published in the United States by
TAN Books
PO Box 269
Gastonia, NC 28053

www.TANBooks.com

Printed in India

Contents

Introduction: The Life and Times of
St. Anselm of Canterbury 1

I. Prayers to the Divine Persons 33

II. Prayers with Mother Mary 57

III. Prayers through the Church Triumphant 93

IV. Prayers and Meditations for the
Church Militant 175

The Life and Times of St. Anselm of Canterbury

Early in his pastoral life, the Church Father St. Augustine (354–430) coined the term "soliloquy" from two Latin words—*solus*, meaning "alone" (where we obviously get words like "solo" and "solitaire") and *loquor*, meaning "to speak" (in words like "loquacious" and "colloquium"). Augustine then named a short treatise *Soliloquies* in order to describe the inner dialogue he had been holding alone with Lady Reason. At the start of this imaginary conversation, Augustine admits that he desires to know God, his own soul, and nothing else—nothing whatsoever. (Augustine: "*Deum et animam scire cupio.*" Reason: "*Nihilne plus?*" Augustine: "*Nihil omnino.*") In this one brief petition, Augustine can be seen setting the groundwork for the medieval mission almost a millennium later.[1]

Known throughout the centuries as the "Second Augustine," Anselm of Canterbury (1033–1109) continued this quest to know both Creator and creature, standing at the threshold of an incredible period of Christian culture. For when Augustine claimed it was essential to know two things, things both heavenly and earthly, he was tasking the Christian mind to know everything possible. As such, he put an end to the pagan claim that "to know thyself" was as far as the mind could go, and he dismissed other religious quests that disparaged the created order so as to know "God alone."

This holding the two tiers of reality together is unique to the Christian faith, which alone can boast the Creator literally becoming a creature, and St. Anselm stands at the cusp of an age that instantiated the effects of this union as boldly and as beautifully as possible. This was the age of Scholasticism, a period of rich intellectual depth marked by the Christian thinker's daring attempt to hold together both God

---

1 St. Augustine of Hippo (d. 430), *Soliloquies* 1.2.7.

and humanity, revelation and reason, nature and grace, intellect and will, the seminary and the university, as well as the Church and the State. This was the recovery of the fact that truth can be found anywhere and truth can never compete against truth. Like a kaleidoscope, both heaven and earth form an interdependent whole where one could meet God only in the world and, in turn, this world was thoroughly charged with the glory of God.

This is the beginning of the High Middle Ages (c. 1000–1500) and the unmatchable intellectual pursuits which gave rise to the great academic works like St. Thomas Aquinas's *Summa Theologiae*, peerless poetry and imagery like Dante's *Divine Comedy*, and architectural wonders like the grand cathedrals of Notre Dame and Chartres, as well as those from Cologne to Canterbury, from Salisbury to Vienna's St. Stephens. It is the age able to finally hold the twin powers of Church and State in a fruitful tension, recognizing how each of the two orders of authority are endowed with their own particular domain and thus governance. It was the age of Christian hymnody, art, and spirituality, an age of the great medieval masterpieces. As such, the term "Middle Ages" should not be disparaged as a convenient filler between two other epochs, say, as only the time between Late Antiquity and the Renaissance, but appreciated for its own unique contributions to the mind's depths as well as the heart's endlessness.

As men of every age, the medieval people thought of themselves as "modern" (*moderni*),[2] but not as many "moderns" do today, that self-regarded cultural elite ungratefully disregarding the past and all her proofs of piety, human decency, and sanity, not to mention sanctity. No, the *moderni* of Anselm's time knew they were the humble debtors of a Christian past and, more importantly, through grace had been made members of a Catholic body which alone was able to harmoniously hold a people together despite the fall of Rome, the rise of barbarism, and the beginnings of early medieval nationalism. As a contemporary of Anselm so famously put it, "We are like dwarfs sitting on the shoulders of giants; we see more things, and things that are further off, than they did—not because our sight is better, or because

---

[2] A phrase used by Richard of St. Victor (1110–73) in the *Prologue* of his *On the Vision of Ezekiel* (*Patrologia Latina* [PL], vol. 196, col. 527).

we are taller than they were, but because they raise us up and add to our stature by their gigantic height."[3]

A Brief Biography of Anselm (1033–1109)

Anselm was born to relatively wealthy landowners in the Burgundian town of Aosta, Italy, in—most likely—April of 1033. Here among the beautiful Alpine mountain range, Anselm and his younger sister, Richeza, experienced both the joys and the stresses of family life.[4] By all accounts, his father, Gundulf, was unaffectionately distant while his mother, Ermenberga, sang of Jesus joyfully and encouraged her children to spend their lives in holy pursuits. Most of what we know about Anselm's life comes only later from the pen of a contemporary

[3] Attributed to Bernard of Chartres (d. c. 1124) in John of Salisbury's (c. 1120–80), *Metalogicon*, a survey of the scholastic curriculum at this time, focusing mainly on the Trivium (the study of grammar, logic, and rhetoric), building upon the quadrivium of arithmetic, astronomy, music, and geometry (Bk. 3.4; PL vol. 199, col. 900).

[4] In a letter to his sister, Richeza (no. 268), Anselm greets her as his only sibling (*unicus frater*), and while other brothers or sisters could have died early in childbirth, these are the only known children of Gundulf and Ermenberga.

historian and friend, Eadmer of Canterbury (1060–1124), who was so impressed with the way his own archbishop carried himself that he composed the *Vita Anselmi*, the *Life of Anselm*.

Anselm took to his mother's strong love of Christ and His Church and was found to be a very studious and intellectually gifted young man. One famous story captures beautifully this intimate familial bond and the family's natural surroundings. Although Gundulf was set on attaining worldly comforts, he allowed his family to have their Catholicism, and Ermenberga worked hard to fill her children's souls with the love of Christ and the sacramentality of all creation, emphasizing how God could be met easily anywhere. This is surely why the young Anselm always imagined God's dwelling to be among the snowcapped Alps, and one night, he dreamt that God Himself had called him to this "higher kingdom," and after a long exchange, God gave Anselm "a piece of the whitest of bread (panis nitidissimus)."[5] Naturally, the young dreamer took this as a call to a priestly

---

[5] From the Latin edition of Eadmer's *Vita Sancti Anselmi* (*Life of St. Anselm*), Bk 1, §2, ed., R. W. Southern (London: Thomas Nelson and Sons, Ltd, 1962), 5.

vocation—a "higher" dwelling and a "lofty" labor, the use of words to convey truth, and the "bread" of Eucharistic communion. This divine invitation was forever stamped in Anselm's psyche. While his father forbade him at age fifteen to enter a school where he would have been trained by monks in the scholastic style, Anselm remained close to Christ. Yet, eventually, Anselm sought distance from his day-to-day life, having grown restless after his mother's death. At the age of twenty-three—sometime in 1056—he crossed the Alps into France and finally made it to the monastic school at Le Bec in Normandy, an intellectual center widely renowned for its scholarly sophistication and led by the brilliant jurist-turned-monk and scholar Lanfranc of Pavia (1005–89).

Under Lanfranc's tutelage, Anselm flourished academically and grew spiritually. Lanfranc's fatherly care and Anselm's love of the intellect rekindled in him the thought of monastic life. Tempted to look neither back nor even around at this point, Anselm was admitted to the Benedictine Monastery of Bec as a novice (1060). Much more amazingly, within only three years, Anselm was nominated prior and the main teacher at the cloister school, Lanfranc having been elevated to abbot of St. Stephen's Abbey in Caen in 1063. For a long time in monastic parlance, the terms "abbot" and "prior" were fairly interchangeable, but as monasteries began to grow in number, the one who had charge over the more practical and logical aspects of religious life was elected for a time as prior; while the abbot, elected for life, served more like a local ordinary (and was thus often mitered), could have charge over more than just one monastery, and was usually involved, *ex officio*, in larger communal and cultural affairs.

As prior (1063–78) overseeing a very busy and full abbey, then, Anselm did much more than just tend to the daily needs of religious life. This was a very fruitful time for him, having somehow carved out time to work on his best-known works: the *Monologion* (1075–76) as well as its "sequel," the *Proslogion* (1077–78), in addition to important treatises dealing with free will, sin, and even the nature of the devil and the problem of evil. These include *On Grammar* (*De grammatico*), *On Truth* (*De Veritate*), *On Free Will* (*De libertate arbitrii*), and *On the Devil's Fall* (*De casu diaboli*). In 1078, Abbot Herluin passed away, and Anselm was unchallenged in succeeding him as the abbot of Bec. This elevation allowed him to travel rather frequently across the English Channel, not only to visit with Lanfranc at Canterbury, who had since been installed as archbishop of Canterbury but also to check in on Bec's local interests there, where devoted, wealthy Norman landowners had bequeathed land and other natural resources to the abbey.

Amidst all these activities and endeavors, Anselm is best known for his "ontological proof," an argument that symbolizes this new way of thinking in the High Middle Ages, a time when a theologian sought to be more than a commentator on sacred Scripture or a collector of insights from earlier Church Fathers. Now, philosophy and argumentation for central Christian truths (like the existence of God) were becoming the means with which Christians could further explore the Faith, defend it from infidels, and open it up for greater evangelical fruit.

Anselm's ontological proof is so named after the Greek word for "being" (*ontos*) and consists of three premises. First, Anselm defines God as "the Being than which no greater being can be conceived" (for if something greater could be imagined, one has not yet come upon God). Second, it is always metaphysically greater to exist in both reality and in the mind than just in the mind alone. (Would you rather have an imaginary $1,000 bill or a real $50 bill?) Therefore, if God is in fact the greatest conceivable being, and it is better to exist in both the mind as well as in the objective world of reality than only in the mind alone, God must exist in both the mind as well as in reality.

This argument not only holds the attention of philosophers and theologians today but also represents Anselm's intellectual contribution to his own times. Anselm wrote a century before Aristotle's main works were rediscovered in the West and translated into Latin, finding full blossom in such giants as Albert the Great (d. 1280) and his student St. Thomas Aquinas (d. 1274). Nonetheless, it was Anselm's embracing of philosophy and the power of human reason which paved the way for this *logica nova*. Although the use of dialectic and reliance on philosophy had only forced some of his contemporaries to deny such central claims as the Eucharist (viz., Berengarius of Tours, d. 1088) and the Trinity (Roscellinus, d. 1121), Anselm's fruitful employment of reason as the handmaid of theology separated him from earlier thinkers who were content simply exegeting the Bible. It also allowed him to help usher in the Aristotelian revolution when that time came.

Accordingly, Anselm's use of human reason in defending, opening up, and advancing divine revelation occasioned a time when men of prayer were also philosophers, when tradesmen were theologians, and when families were understood to be the first fonts of heavenly grace. This is how we are to make sense of a monk and bishop who is also invoked as the "Father of Scholasticism," as Anselm strove never to isolate or to confuse faith and reason, humble enough to find and use truth wherever and however it appeared.

In 1089, Archbishop Lanfranc of Canterbury died, and afraid of being named his immediate successor, Anselm paused any travels to England. However, in 1092, he gave in to some pressing messages received from an ailing friend and influential earl on how best to establish a new monastery at St. Werburgh's. This trip was exploited by the local populace there to convince Anselm to take the See of Canterbury, officially nominating him in the spring of 1093 and forcibly putting the bishop's crozier in his hands and carrying him to a local church. Anselm countered by saying he could not abandon Bec and his duties there, but by summer, he had used his obvious resistance to the Church's advantage—pressuring King William to agree to the central tenets of the Gregorian Reform, to return any land the crown had recently seized from the Church, and to confess Urban II (d. 1099) as the rightful pope and thus condemn Guibert of Ravenna, a.k.a. "Pope" Clement III (d. 1100), as an antipope. This caused further negotiations, and although Anselm did not receive everything for which he asked, he felt enough had been rightfully returned to the Church and accepted the archbishopric of Canterbury on September 25, 1093, surprisingly causing William to finally acquiesce to the conditions he had not previously accepted.

After six years of shepherding his flock, years filled with pastoral as well as theological fruit, Anselm died on April 21, 1109, which today marks his feast day. He was canonized in 1494, proclaimed a Doctor of the Church by Pope Clement XI in 1720, and has been named the patron saint of philosophers and theologians.

Anselm's Theology of Justice and Honor

As the consummate fulfillment of Judaism, Christianity is a creed based not on a contract of goods but on a covenant between persons. A contract is a *quid pro quo*—a this for that. It is what the ancients called *do ut des*—I give you this, so you give me that. But that is not how the one true God behaves. What could creatures ever give Him which He does not have? For that reason, God is ever faithful, even (especially?) when His people stray (e.g., after the great flood, "the Lord said to Himself: 'Never again will I curse the ground because of human beings, since the desires of the human heart are evil from youth; nor will I ever again strike down every living being, as I have done.'" Gn 8:21). This is the theological backdrop behind each and every one of Anselm's writings.

Because humanity could never make amends or atone to God for His faithfulness, Anselm has to find another source of divine satisfaction, and nowhere is his unique sense of justice and honor more apparent than in this work on *Why God Became Man* (*Cur Deus Homo*; composed 1097–98). Here, the archbishop breaks from most of the patristic tradition and refuses to attribute the Incarnation to a battle between God and the devil.

That is, whereas most of the Church Fathers understood salvation as Jesus the strongman conquering Satan and ransoming the human race back from him (cf. Mt 20:28; Mk 10:45), Anselm found the devil having any contractual "rights" over God's creatures to be an outrageous claim upon the Lord's absolute and unchallengeable sovereignty. Instead, Anselm places the drama within God's very own self. When Adam (and, in him, the entire human race) turned from God and incurred the punishment of death, a great—no, the perfect—Lord was affronted and defrauded of the eternal honor due to Him. How, then, would such an offense be made right?

Timeless thinkers like Anselm are also products of their own culture. It should therefore be no surprise to see how the core tenets of feudalism reverberate throughout his doctrine of atonement: to rectify, and make amends for, God's broken honor, out of love for subservient sinners, the Son takes on mortal flesh in order to offer the ultimate act of obedience on behalf of a class of ungrateful subordinates—God's own death, death on a Cross. This bloody sacrifice sets the order of justice aright, and Anselm draws on his theology of justice and the role of fittingness to defend the Incarnation and all of Jesus's life-giving actions.

Cur Deus Homo begins by reminding readers how each and every human soul has been made in God's image and likeness and has thus been created to choose eternal blessedness (cf. Gn 1:27; Gn 2:7). Because of our pride and an enamoration with our own God-given splendor, we rejected such a graced invitation for further communion. Consequently, humanity's sin must be atoned for, but no descendant of Adam is now good or honorable enough to make such satisfaction. Only God can do that. So, if it is fitting that man makes satisfaction, and it is unfitting that God—the only One Who could actually succeed in doing so—makes such satisfaction, what, then, is a suitable solution? Anselm's answer is that it is most fitting and most beautiful (given the order of justice) that a God Man atone for man's affront to God, thereby honoring God's original intent in bringing humanity into beatitude, and thus avoiding the impossible—that the plans of an omnipotent God ever be frustrated.

Such an explanation saves both divine mercy and divine justice. It is merciful that an insulted Sovereign open a way to make things right again; it is just that God neither simply ignores the wrong nor somehow makes satisfaction Himself. The truth, the beauty, and the justice of all reality thus demands that a God-made-Man intercede and atone to God on behalf of Man, both of which the Son freely is. This sense of restoring honor and dignity runs throughout the prayers below as well. No sinner has the absolute right to approach a God Whom he has killed, and God's justice does not demand His entering into a covenant with this rebellious race. Yet out of the Incarnation's mercy, the Son reestablishes God's original order of justice by graciously and forgivingly bringing mortals back into His eternal blessedness.

Anselm's Theology of Prayer

Given this sense of divine satisfaction, Anselm knew that a creature's talking to its Creator is audacious. Prayer is daring, something we hear at every Mass: "At the Savior's command and formed by divine teaching, *we dare* to say (*audemus dicere*)." And this is precisely why Anselm dare not approach God alone but, instead, invokes the help of all the saints. In fact, as we shall see, everything Anselm highlights in his prayers is ultimately God's doing, God's gift entrusted to a particular person and thus lived out in his or her own personality, life's experiences, and concrete historical period. In this way, prayer for Anselm really does prove to be God's descent into a soul contrite enough to allow that mutual indwelling, and then the Lord finally has the fallen soul's "permission" to be lifted out of its despondency into the heavenly life.

That is why constant throughout the following prayers is Anselm's sense of self-abasement, a radically expressed sense of contrition which may not easily land on Christian ears today. The violence obvious in each prayer highlights the distance between God's perfection and our wretchedness (*miser*, the Latin term Anselm uses most often to describe the state of his soul). That is why at the heart of every prayer is a call for compunction, a piercing of the fallen heart which must not be caused simply by self-deprecation but by a heavenly love which would otherwise shatter the human soul if it were not made more pliable through penance.

As such, sorrow, contrition, and a deep owning of our own fragility are all present at the onset of each prayer, as the sinner stands unadorned before the Almighty. Yet, like the Holy Mass Anselm celebrated daily as priest and bishop (and of which we still remain recipients), the penitential rite is only the beginning of worship—it may commence our communal praise of God, but it does so only to make room for further illumination (Liturgy of the Word) and then the ultimate goal of divine-human communion (Liturgy of the Eucharist). This is how we must read Anselm's sense of deep and personal sorrow which at times can look like an ungodly self-loathing. Where he is introspectively harsh with himself, we are forced to admit some hyperbole, but we also want to appreciate the theology of his indebtedness.

Anselm was one who deeply and completely took to heart Jesus's words that, "I am the vine, you are the branches. Whoever remains in me and I in him will bear much fruit, because *without me you can do nothing*" (Jn 15:5). Unlike most, Anselm certainly did not suffer from any sense of spiritual entitlement, realizing that without Jesus, it is *not* that he could not accomplish something grand, *not* that he could not perform miracles—it is that without Jesus, he knew he could do absolutely *nothing*. Do you really believe that? Perhaps most of us pray and call for the presence of Christ usually as an afterthought, only when our plans are in peril or when we feel in need of "extra" help. But as we shall see, the real power of Anselm's prayers comes through his awareness that everything depends on Jesus and that even a saintly scholar, monk, or archbishop has no good, no merit, no accomplishment of his own. All is Jesus's doing, and it is here his sense of deep abasement begins.

The following prayers belong to a collection that was unique among medieval collections in that it was the first to circulate under its known author, penned with Anselm's name and not anonymously or piously under a pseudonym or the patronage of some ancient saint. We can only imagine how this collection of prayers came to be: certainly, alone in Anselm's soul as he prayed in the chapel and in his cell. However, being known for his approachability and generosity, he was asked to share the fruits of this contemplation with a pious woman, Adelaide, one of the ten children born to William the Conqueror. Such an exchange was not uncommon between well-known churchmen and nobles (especially "great ladies" like Adelaide) who were longing to grow in Christian holiness but lacked the theological training and the realistic resources which would work well with their state in life.

In his exchange with Adelaide, Archbishop Anselm writes (*Epistle* 10) that he will send seven prayers and some reflections on the Psalms (which he called *Flores Psalmorum—Flowers of the Psalms*—which have not survived, highlighting the importance of the prayers which were copied and distributed widely). He is doing this so Adelaide's heart might tend toward a more burning charity (*ad accendendum amorem*) of God and that through the rigorous introspection the prayers demand, she may more despise her sins by desiring to grow more humble, by humbling, experience the terror of her final judgment and that such a moment of distress might result in groans and tears (*gemitus et lacrymas*). Even to one so lofty and so influential, Anselm keeps the pattern of prayer he himself experienced in private: only in darkness can we finally see the light, only in self-abasement can we be lifted upward, and only in tears and groaning can the joy of heaven be forever ours.

Anselm's freely and so openly sharing his prayer life with another helps us see how he must have always thought of his conversations with God as a communal event, knowing how we are all surrounded by that "great cloud of witnesses" (Heb 12:1) and that the graces of prayer are meant for everyone. For in each of his prayers, Anselm searches for a point of contact between the saint's experience and our lives as well. For instance, Paul can relate to our slow journey to conversion, Peter is sympathetic with those who betray the Christ, Mary Magdalene knows what it is like to be misunderstood, and all have friends and enemies whom they must love and for whom they must offer prayer. So, when you pray the prayers that follow, seek to know each saint in the manner described by Anselm. These were real people not much different than ourselves, yet people who placed Jesus above all else and placed all else—their families and friends, their careers and finances, their romances and their pastimes—in Jesus.

The original collection of Anselm's prayers consisted of nineteen in all: one is to God in general, three are directed toward Jesus, three to the Blessed Virgin Mary, ten to various saints for various situations, and one prayer for his friends as well as one for his enemies. There are also three longer theological meditations treating some core tenet of the Christian drama.

Anselm's Devotion to Mother Mary

Included in this collection of prayers are found three petitions intended to be united to the perfect prayers of Mary, the Mother of God. Anselm lived at the cusp of a time of great Marian devotion, an age when the theological intricacies of both the Immaculate Conception as well as the Assumption were being worked out, as these feasts were slowly being celebrated across monasteries and churches in Europe. In 1060, for example, a feast commemorating the mystery of Mary's conception into this world was celebrated throughout most of England with a special liturgy. In 1066, however, this feast was abolished under William the Conqueror but was reinstated just a generation later. This liturgy honored the popular pieties that sought to celebrate Mary's being brought into this world by means of unmatched divine activity.

Anselm never doubted Mary's divine motherhood or her virginity, even composing a treatise in 1099 entitled *On the Virginal Conception and Original Sin* (*De Conceptu Virginali et de Peccato Originali*). He most often drew on the ancient title *Mater Dei*, the Mother of God; he invokes her as the Mother of the human race, he summons her as the Advocatrix—a female advocate in collaboration with the Holy Spirit, *the* Advocate—and sees how next to God, she is the holiest of all, the greatest of all Marys. But Mary's sinlessness was a challenge for a mind which wondered what one immaculately conceived would do to Christianity's claim that Jesus Christ came to save all.

In other words, Anselm could not hold (1) that the Son of God came to die to save *everyone* if (2) there were in fact a human who herself was sinless. In an amazing twist of fate, this question was answered by Anselm's student and biographer Eadmer (whose writings would later be wrongly attributed to

Anselm himself, ironically bolstering the Church's embracing of the Immaculate Conception). Eadmer knew that Mary was saved, "My soul proclaims the greatness of the Lord, my spirit rejoices in God *my Savior*" (Lk 1:46), but what Eadmer worked out in a way that Anselm could not was how Mary was not just redeemed but was "pre-redeemed," saved by the mercy of God at the very same time she was conceived in the womb of her mother.

By using Anselm's own theological sequencing on why the Incarnation was the most fitting way to save the world, Eadmer first laid out that whatever God does, He does not just in a way that is good or better than other means but in the best way possible. The Son of God therefore becomes human in the most excellent being possible: born uniquely of a physical virgin and, if possible, a virgin who herself is also spiritually virginal—that is, sinless. Because it is most fitting that God do what is best and because it is possible that one could be brought into the world without original sin (e.g., Adam and Eve), it is most excellent that the Mother of God was conceived immaculately. Little did Eadmer know that in defending the local customs and liturgical calendars of English monasteries and parishes, he was also setting the stage for other thinkers like Duns Scotus (d. 1308) and, eventually, Pope Pius IX in 1854 to promulgate the universal dogma of the Immaculate Conception.

How to Use These Pages

TAN Books has chosen to issue this volume of an updated translation of those prayers and meditations where the soul's journey from sin to sanctity is the clearest. In some ways, Anselm continues what we might call an Augustinian existentialism. Anselm can relate to the more modern term "existentialist" because he feels deeply the dreadful search for ultimate meaning that every rational mortal must face. Every prayer and meditation thus begins with the most profound questions (for which the modern existentialist, like Albert Camus or Jean-Paul Sartre, had no real answer): What is this life all about? Why do I continue to struggle with moments of meaninglessness? Why do I continue to do what I really do not want to do? Why is there such decay and death all around? Yet these existentialist questions are, more importantly, also "Augustinian" in nature because—like his patristic predecessor—Anselm knows where to go to make sense of these questions. Only Jesus Christ, a scarred and crucified God Who has freely suffered the Cross to raise the sinner to the sanctified, can answer the deepest questions of human existence.

Jesus does not simply provide answers, He is the Answer—"the Way and the Truth and the Life" (Jn 14:6). Jesus came not to give direction and lessons but to give His very Self. As the history of God's first Chosen People proves, the Law is never enough. This is why the prayers and meditations of Anselm are so visceral, so intimate, so personal. He writes not only to produce a picture of a loving Savior but to bring that Savior into the soul through prayerful reading and ponderous contemplation.

As such, TAN Books asks that you take your time to pray through whatever words of Anselm resonate with you. Or as St. Anselm himself wrote so carefully in the first *Preface* to this collection of prayers:

The prayers and meditations written down below are meant to arouse the reader's mind toward either the love or the fear of God, or perhaps to deeper self-awareness. These should not be read while your soul is in tumult. Instead, do so in quiet—and do so neither skimming nor rushing, but take just a little at a time in deep meditation. Nor should you, the reader, feel a need to read any one of these in its entirety. Pray over as much as you feel you are able, and with God's grace, use whatever you have read to kindle in you a prayerful spirit as much as you can. Moreover, it is not necessary for you to always start at the beginning, but start wherever you feel most called. For this reason, the paragraphs are separated into smaller parts, so that you may begin or pause wherever you choose. In this way the lengthiness or the frequent repetition of the same passage should not seem wearisome, but hopefully you, the reader, may receive a greater desire to ponder piously these words that follow.

Note the three possible outcomes Anselm sees in one's spiritual life: fear of God, love of God, and a growth in self-awareness.

First, of course, the biblical sanction to fear God is where we begin to order reality properly: "Fear of the Lord is the beginning of knowledge; fools despise wisdom and discipline" (Prv 1:7). The foolish might fear God for what He can do, but the wise "fear" God simply for Who He is and thus have more of an awe or an unearthly reverence for the Almighty. To pay Him homage and to seek to live as He—your Creator—asks is the essence of piety, that kind of admiration and amazement that One so great has chosen not only to create you but to love you and even to rely on you to extend His kingdom. After fear comes Anselm's hope that these prayers will also lead to a greater love of God, clearly the goal on which everyone's salvation pivots. This love is the very definition of who God is (cf. 1 Jn 4:8). But by becoming human, this Love has become our neighbor, and that is why, for the Christian, "if we love one another, God remains in us, and his love is brought to perfection in us" (1 Jn 4:12).

A beautiful circle emerges: to love God, one must love one's neighbor, and to love one's neighbor truly is to love God. The third goal is a greater awareness of one's own soul. Self-examination and the awareness of one's intentions and deepest desires are Anselm's way of reminding us that we all have a role to play in our own salvation. Ultimately, we shall all get what we really want: heaven or hell, and that is why it is imperative to know one's soul and to constantly bring what lies underneath to the light. For this, Anselm prefers to use a saint as our soul's mirror and see in that holy one of God our own hidden faults, embarrassing sins, and our holiest yearnings.

In Anselm's prayers and meditations, we meet a man who knows deeply the nausea of depravity and can oftentimes sound like one filled with nothing but self-loathing. Yet this existential angst never has the last word but serves as a spur to let down all his defenses and to allow the Lord to embrace Anselm as he is—a sinner yet called to surrender to sanctity. It is always tempting to think that famous churchmen were always pious and faithful and never struggled with the doubts and despair sin inevitably ushers into a soul. We should always remember that only one saint in the Catholic Tradition was so since conception; apart from Mother Mary, the other saints in the Mystical Body knew, like each of us do, the cycle of sin, contrition, conversion over and over again.

Ponder each prayer slowly and pause to contemplate particularly fruitful passages. Each prayer begins with a brief introduction and is then broken up to facilitate your prayerful lingering. Each prayer ends with three questions and suggestions for further reading if you find the images and movements of that particular prayer especially fruitful for your soul. You might consider keeping a pen or pencil and a journal next to you as you ponder Anselm's words, keeping a record of what you find important, challenging, or alluring enough to return to later in more depth.

A Final Note on the Text and Translation

As we saw with the Marian treatise once attributed to Anselm, over the centuries, many otherwise unknown devotional writings were conveniently attached to his works. This was a move not unique to the archbishop of Canterbury: great writers with a distinct style and sound tended to attract that hard-to-place piece, that homily without a known author, that loose page on the floor of the medieval scriptorium, and so on. How many prayers and sayings are "attributed" to such great minds and hearts like Saints Augustine, Teresa of Avila, or Ignatius of Loyola but cannot be located anywhere in their critical writings? For that reason, TAN Books has included excerpts from the nineteen known prayers of St. Anselm and selections from only two of his twenty-one lengthier *Meditations*, as the best of critical scholarship recognizes only *Meditations* one to three as authentic.

Working from various Latin editions, our team of translators and theologians first went and put Anselm's words into a verbatim, literal English version. After that accomplishment, this literal text was prayerfully rendered into a more readable and accessible English, sometimes adding a name to clarify a pronoun or even explaining a more theological term with further clarification in order to help modern readers to continue their prayer and understanding. Because Anselm has a tendency to switch addressees rapidly and without warning in his prayers—say, talking to Mary at one point and then in the very next line addressing his own sins or God's good creation—all references to any of the divine persons were capitalized—He, Him, His; You, Yours—in order to help keep the one (or One) to whom (or Whom) he was praying clear.

I.

Prayers to the Divine Persons

Prayer to God

This opening prayer, considered the most important in Anselm's collection, is a simple plea for a sinner to be forgiven, to grow in self-awareness, and then to be open to the graces for serious spiritual battle, aiming toward the theological virtues ("belief, hope, love"). Amidst the Anselmian tendency to beg for humility and mortification is the crucial awareness that love is all that matters and the only life for which all will be judged: "All I really want is to love You." As a faithful churchman, Anselm sees the inextricable link between such charity and the teachings of Christ, commands which must not only be lived out but lived freely and joyfully. In other words, from the start, the love Anselm seeks has "rules" and practical guidelines and concrete criteria.

Almighty God, tender Father and good Lord, have mercy on me, a sinner (see Lk 18:13). Forgive my sins. Grant me to be cautious and even conquer all the traps, temptations, and toxic treats in my life. In both my thoughts and in my actions, may I perfectly avoid what You forbid and do what You command. May I believe, hope, love, and live in accord with Your mind and will. Grant me a contrite piety, a humility, and the ability to live abstemiously and to mortify my flesh (cf. Rom 8:13).

All I really want is to love You, to pray to You, to praise You, and to meditate upon You. In all things, may I act according to Your will with purity of heart, solemnity of mind, devotion, and with a mind made true and useful.

Allow me to know Your teachings and to love them, delight in them, and to follow them easily and fruitfully. Always, Lord, let me never grow slothful but advance humbly in life toward higher and higher things. Never let me rely, Lord, on my human ignorance, my own weakness, nor on my own merits, never allow me to trust anything other than Your own dutiful disposition towards me. Treat me mercifully and use all my thoughts and deeds in accord with Your loving will (cf. Mt 6:10) so that Your plan may always be accomplished in me and by me. Free me from every evil and lead me to eternal life through the Lord (cf. Mt 6:13).

Questions for Prayerful Reflection

- Do you tend to pray to God in general or more specifically to the Father, Son, or Holy Spirit?
- When you pray with Anselm's words here, are you able to understand your sins in the context of God's love, or do you tend to condemn yourself and find yourself unable to approach Him? That is, when speaking to God, do you tend to stay away from those images and memories of your life you find embarrassing or uncomfortable?
- When you approach God in prayer, what do you "rely" on—your supposed virtues, your successes, your talents and gifts, or do you come to God more honestly, relying only on His grace and goodness?

Prayer to Christ When the Mind Longs to Burn with His Love

After the opening prayer to the Godhead in general, the next three prayers of Anselm are offered to the Second Person of the Divine Trinity in particular. These three prayers are to the God-made-flesh, Jesus Christ—to His Person (no. 2), more specifically to His Body and Blood (no. 3), and then to a representation of Christ's Cross (no. 4). In the following prayer, "When the Mind Longs to Burn with [Jesus's] Love," Anselm invites us to place ourselves before Jesus and see how great is His generosity, especially as compared to how little we truly desire to be totally His. As such, this is the first set of prayers where Anselm's theology of honor plays a crucial role. The Lord's love will forever outrun the degree to which we are indebted to Him: "I in no way have come to love You as much as I owe You." Yet in a spirit of courage and filial trust, Anselm perseveres in begging the Lord to decrease this disparity between His perfect care and the sinner's lukewarm indifference. Notice here how prayer for Anselm (and for any saint) is never a compartmentalized moment of an otherwise busy day. Notice how very "sensual" this prayer is: all of Anselm's being is taken up praising a Christ he sees, feels, listens to, and whose banquet he cannot wait to taste. Does Jesus pervade your world in such glory, surround your experiences with such richness?

Lord Jesus Christ, my Redemption, my Mercy, my Salvation: I praise You and I give You thanks. Yet how wholly unequal is my piety compared to Your generosity and how much more is expected of true devotion. How absolute is the meagerness of my desire, how lavish is the sweetness of Your charity. Regardless of the little sort of praise and thanks which I realize are in no way equal to what I owe You, but insofar as I am able, my soul will fulfill its debt to You.

Since You are the hope of my heart, the strength of my soul, the cure for my infirmity, may Your most powerful tenderness take care of what my most tepid stupidity tries to accomplish. You are my life and the goal of my desire, even though I in no way have come to love You as much as I owe You, let my desire to love You match how much I should actually love You. My Light, You see the inner recesses of my soul because, "My Lord, my deepest yearning is before You" (Ps 38:10), and You have graced my soul with any good it desires.[6] If You inspire all that

---

[6] This is sometimes a difficult truth to realize but it is solid Christian teaching that any desire for the good in any fallen soul is a gift of God. God places holy desires in us, and in so doing, His gifts become our merits. In *Preface I* for the *Mass of the*

is good, Lord, or better, You inspire it because it is good,[7] I thus desire to love You.

Saints, the priest prays, "For You are praised in the company of Your Saints and, in crowning their merits, You crown Your own gifts." This Preface is very "Augustinian": "God thus crowns you because he crowns his own gifts (*dona sua*) and not your merits (*merita tua*)" (*Expositions of the Psalms*, 102.7). The Augustinian tradition worked this teaching out against the heresy of Pelagianism, named after the monk Pelagius, who wrongly taught that there can be good in a soul apart from God's direct act of grace and each person can increase that good through harder and harder work. The truth is that without God's grace, we cannot only not do good, we "can do nothing" (Jn 15:5).

7 Here Anselm echoes what has been called "The Euthyphro Problem," which he certainly knew from his philosophy studies. It is so-called because the seemingly unsolvable problem in question was first posed in Plato's dialogue on piety, *The Euthyphro*. Plato's dilemma is the question whether (1) something is good because it is willed by God or (2) does God will something because it is good? If one sides with the first possibility, one falls into the problem of moral relativism in that God could will anything (e.g., the torture of the innocent) and we would be bound to call anything "good." All commands and basic moral instincts would be emptied of any real meaning. But, if one sides with the second possibility, God is no longer the sovereign Good but must bow to an independent order of goodness, and we would be caught up in a sort of cosmic dualism. Here God wills something because it has a claim on Him, and not as the sovereign Creator Who brings all things into being (and thus into goodness, as we shall see). Clearly, neither horn of this dilemma is acceptable, and it would fall to St. Thomas Aquinas to clarify how goodness is synonymous with God's very nature and is not something He

Complete in me what You have created me to desire, granting that I may come to love You as much as You ask.[8] I offer You praise and thanks for this desire which You have inspired within me; I offer praise and prayers, lest this gift which you have granted through your own goodness proves unfruitful. Perfect what You have started and bring to completion what You have created me to be, not because of my merits, but because of Your goodness which goes before all else.

Transform, Most Merciful One, my lukewarmness into an exceedingly fervent love for You. This, most clement God, is what my prayer seeks: that remembering these things and meditating on Your kindnesses, I might be illumined by Your love. Your

---

simply wills apart from Himself. God is not just a "good," He is Goodness, and, therefore, He is the Bestower, the Standard, and the supreme Exemplar of all good. Nothing outside God binds Him but all things are now bound to Him and, as such, all things are metaphysically good insofar as they exist.

8 Anselm rightly prays to have an upright will, to desire what is truly desirable. The Christian problem is not one of the intellect; we sin not because we fail to know deep dogma or are unable to articulate the Creed like Oxford dons. The real problem lies in our wills, in not wanting to belong fully to Christ and, instead, wanting what is harmful for our eternal well-being. This is surely why God becomes a helpless Child, a gentle Teacher, a crucified God—to win our wills over through gentleness and to melt the chilly indifference of our hearts through weakness.

goodness created me, Lord, and Your mercy has cleansed what You had made from original sin. Your patience has carried me thus far—even after I floundered in my sordid sinfulness, having lost that baptismal cleansing. Yours is a patience that sustains me and has waited for me. That is, Good Lord, You await my reformed life while my soul waits for a sufficient repentance so that through the inbreathing (*inspirationem*) of Your grace, it might live well with You.[9]

My Lord, my Creator, my Patience, and my Nourisher, be also my Helper. For You, I thirst, hunger, and desire; for You, I sigh; for You, I long. I am like an orphan who has been stripped of the closeness of a most tender father, crying and bawling, unceasingly and wholeheartedly longing to embrace his loving face.[10] As much as I can—although this

---

[9] This section of Anselm's prayer emphasizes our ongoing need for God's mercy and our own awareness that repentance never ceases before one's death. For even though the sacrament of Baptism cleanses the stain of original sin, our own freely chosen aversion to God thereafter stands in need of constant healing. Finally, the Latin here is our word for "inspire," a breathing into, and clearly Anselm's intentional reference to the Holy Spirit's indwelling, the teaching that the same Spirit Who indwelt Jesus now inhabits the soul of every baptized believer.

[10] While this may sound harsh and cold, know that in the

is not as much as I ought—I contemplate Your Passion and remember Your beatings, Your scourgings, Your Cross, and I remember Your wounds, and how You were put to death for me, and how Your body was anointed, buried, but at the same time I recall Your glorious resurrection and miraculous ascension. I hold all these things with an unwavering faith, bemoaning my state of exile (cf. Eph 2:19) and hoping in the one consolation, Your return, and so I burn to gloriously behold Your face.

Pitiful me because I was not able to see the Lord of angels lowered to converse with men, empowering men to converse with angels. A rejected God freely died so a sinner could live. Alas, I was too unworthy to be astonished in the actual presence of something so admirable, something so immeasurably loving. Oh my soul, why were you not present when the sword of intense sorrow ran through you (cf. Lk 2:35)? Why were you unable to be wounded

---

Prologue to the Benedictine *Rule*, St. Benedict sought to inspire his monks toward holiness by telling them that "we must serve God always with the talents He has given us so that He will refuse to disinherit us, His children, like an angry father, nor infuriated by our sinfulness that He would give us over to eternal torments like a fearsome Lord."

by the iron lance which pierced the side of your Savior (cf. Jn 19:34a)? Why were you found unworthy to see the nails puncture the hands and the feet of your Creator (cf. Jn 20:20)? Why did you turn away in horror from the blood pouring out from your Redeemer (Jn 19:34b)? Why were you not inebriated with seething tears when He was given bitter gall to drink (cf. Lam 3:15; Mt 27:34)? Why did you not compassionately accompany the most chaste Virgin, His most worthy Mother, and your most loving matron?

My most merciful Lady, how could I describe the fountains which sprung forth from your most chaste eyes when you beheld your only Son before you, innocent but bound, beaten, and butchered? What might I presume about the torrent of tears that poured down your most loving face when you looked up to see your own Son and God and Lord hanging on the cross, the flesh of your flesh cruelly torn apart by faithless men? How could I ever estimate what weeping plagued your most pure heart when you heard, "Woman, behold your Son" (Jn 19:26), and when the disciple heard, "Behold your mother" (Jn 19:27)? For in the place of your Son, you received a disciple in place of the Master, a servant instead of the Lord.

If only I could have taken my Lord down from that cross along with blessed Joseph of Arimathea, prepared His body with spices, and laid Him in the tomb (see Jn 19:38–42)! Or even if I could have come afterwards so that such a burial would not have been without my grieving. If only I could have been among that blessed chorus of women, trembling at the sight of angels and hearing the announcement of my Lord's resurrection, the news of my own consolation, the news of that which has been so long awaited and so, so desired! If only I could have heard from the mouth of the angel, "Do not be afraid, Jesus who was crucified whom you seek is risen, he is not here" (Mt 28:5).

Kindest, Sweetest, Most Peaceful One, when will You make up for the fact that I did not witness the blessed incorruption of Your Body? How will I ever place a kiss on the wounded places where those nails pierced You? Will I ever be able to bedew with tears of joy those scars that prove You are truly flesh and bones (cf. Lk 24:39)? Admirable, Inestimable, and

Incomparable One, when will You console me and when will You lessen my pain?

For such pain cannot subside while I am still on pilgrimage and far from the Lord. Cursed is my soul, Lord, because You, my life's Consoler, have ascended but have not said goodbye. Ascending, You blessed those who were in your company, but I was not there. "With raised hands" (Lk 24:50) You were taken up into heaven by a cloud, but I did not see this. Angels promised You would one day return, but this I did not hear.

So, what shall I say? What shall I do? Where shall I go? Where should I look for Him? Where and when might I find Him? Whom shall I ask? Who can speak to me of my Beloved, "for I languish with love" (Sg 2:5; 5:8)? "Joy has been drained from my heart and my laughter has been changed into weeping" (Lam 5:15). "My flesh and my heart fail me, God is the rock of my heart, my portion forever" (Ps 73:26). Unless it comes from You, my Dearest One, "my soul refuses to be consoled" (Ps 77:3). "Whom else have I in the heavens? None beside You delights me on earth" (Ps 73:25). I want You, I hope in You, it is You I seek. "My heart spoke to You, saying, 'Seek my face, Your face, Lord, I seek! Do not hide Your face from me'" (Ps 27:8–9).

Kindliest Lover of all peoples, "To You the helpless entrust their cause, You are the defender of orphans" (Ps 10:14; Lam 5:3). My most reliable Advocate, have mercy on this abandoned orphan. For I have become a fatherless orphan, my soul has become like that of a widow.[11] Look at these, the tears of an orphan and a widow, which is all I can offer You until You return. Hurry, Lord, show Yourself, and then I shall be consoled. "Show me Your face and I shall be saved" (Ps 80:20). Make Your presence known and I shall obtain my heart's desire. Reveal Your glory and my joy will be made perfect. "For You my body yearns; for You my soul thirsts" (Ps 63:2). "My soul thirsts for God, the living God. When can I enter and see the face of God?" (Ps 42:3) When will You come, my Consoler, Whom I await? Oh, when shall I see my joy for which I long? Oh, if only "I could be satisfied when Your glory appears" (Ps 17:15), for which I hunger. Oh, then shall I become intoxicated "feasting on the rich

[11] Here Anselm is placing himself in the place of those for whom God has a special affection: "Father of the fatherless, defender of widows" (Ps 68:6).

food of Your house" (Ps 36:9a), for which I long; if only You would give me to drink "from Your delightful stream" (Ps 36:9b), for which I thirst.

Lord, let my "tears be my bread day and night" (Ps 42:4) until it is said to me: "Behold your God," until I hear, "Awake, soul, here is your Bridegroom" (Mt 25:6). But in this meantime, feed me with sorrows and let me drink my tears, and let my sorrows be my comforts. Maybe then my Redeemer will come, since He is good; He will not delay because He is loving. To Him give the glory forever and ever. Amen.

Questions for Prayerful Reflection

- Think of that which you hold most dear in your life—your family, your friends, your talents and passions, the highlights of your life's story, and so on. Now imagine all those treasures as God's direct gifts to you—not things of your own doing, not the results of your own intelligence and connections, but gifts pure and simple. How does that help you see things more truthfully?

- What would it mean for you to "fervently love" God, as Anselm pleads throughout?
- Imagine yourself at the foot of the Cross on that first Good Friday, AD 33. What would you say to Jesus; what would you feel? What do you hear; whom do you see? Now imagine yourself at the empty tomb three days later. What would you feel; what would you want Jesus to know about you?

Prayer for Receiving the Body and Blood of the Lord

Holy Communion is, of course, the way Jesus Christ—God made flesh—continues His promise to never leave us orphans (cf. Jn 14:18) and to be with us always, even until the end of time (cf. Mt 28:20). Anselm's prayer before receiving the Sacred Host (number three in his collection) begins by placing the redemption of the world in the plan of the Father's sending the Son in the power of the Holy Spirit. This collaborative work continues in the celebration of Holy Mass: the priest calls down the Holy Spirit as the Sacred Host is then offered to the Father, involving all believers in this heavenly elevation. As such, Anselm prays that this liturgy becomes his own, transforming how he feels, how he speaks, and how he lives.

Lord, Jesus Christ, Who by the orchestration of the Father and the work of the Holy Spirit, through Your freely-willed death, You so mercifully redeemed this world from sin and eternal death. I adore You and I venerate You as much I seem able, despite how tepid my affection and lowly my devotion—giving You thanks for such a gift, Your Holy Body and Your Holy Blood which I desire to receive as a cleansing of my sins as well as a defense against them.

I confess, Lord, that I am not worthy to come near (cf. Lk 7:6) and even touch this Sacrament, but I place my trust in that same tenderness toward sinners with which You handed over Your soul so that they may be justified, and by which You offered Yourself as a holy sacrifice unto the Father. A sinner, I believe I may accept these gifts so I too may be justified by them. I beg and beseech You, Merciful Lover of Mankind: let what You have given for the wiping away of sins never prove to increase my sins but serve to absolve them and act as a protection against them.

Lord, make me discerning in mouth and in heart, that I might know by faith and by heartfelt affection, that through the power of these Sacraments, I am empowered to be conformed to Your death and resurrection. [Through the power of these Sacraments], through the death of the "old man," and through a renewal of my faith-life (cf. Rom 6:6), may I be made worthy to be incorporated into Your Body, "which is the Church" (Col 1:24). Then I am your member and You are my Head, and I will remain in You and You in me (cf. Jn 15:4). Then at Your resurrection, You will reform my "lowly body" and configure it to Your spiritual body (cf. Phil 3:21; 1 Cor 15:39–49), according to the promise of Your apostle, and then I shall forever rejoice in You unto Your glory, You Who live and reign with the Father and the Holy Spirit, God forever and ever. Amen.

Questions for Prayerful Reflection

- Pray this prayer before receiving Holy Communion next. What words or images most resonate with you?
- Do you understand how Communion is also a Sacrifice? In elevating the Host to the Father, the priest is showing you how Jesus the Lamb is perpetually lifting

you up to God and in so doing, forgiving your sins through His Blood and thus raising you into the life of heaven even here and now.

- Imagine yourself as a living member of Christ's own Sacred Body. You are His hands and eyes, His words and His heart while on earth. Holy Communion grafts and strengthens that union every time you receive the Host. Where does such intimacy call you toward greater holiness in your day-to-day life?

Prayer to the Holy Cross

The Cross is the sign of salvation, for here the Son's sacrifice absolves what sinful humanity has justly incurred, a sacrifice received and ratified come Easter Morning. This prayer of St. Anselm, number four, is essentially unique from other medieval prayers to the Cross, for it is offered not simply to the actual Cross of Calvary but to whatever crucifix is before him, as simple or as plain as it might be. Consequently, these words were written for his contemporaries (and for us) as a way to pray before the crucifix in one's own home or at the local parish. In doing so, pay attention to what comes to mind, the people you remember and the feelings that surface as you actually speak to the cross before you, imagining Jesus dying out of love for you.[12] *This prayer reminds us that we must all have a special place in our home where a crucifix is clearly visible and where we have our own prayer time.*

Oh holy cross, which brings that Cross upon which our Lord Jesus Christ perished so as to rescue us from the eternal death toward which we were all heading, and into the eternal life which we had lost because of our sinning: I adore you, I venerate you, and in you I glorify that one Cross which you symbolize for us, and on that Cross I adore, venerate, and glorify the Lord's compassion worked so mercifully there.

Oh, loveable cross on which is our salvation, our life and our resurrection! Oh, precious wood through which we have been saved, through which we have been freed. Oh, venerable sign through which we have been set apart for God! Oh, glorious cross in whom alone we should boast!

---

[12] For clarity's sake, Cross has been capitalized when referring to the actual wood on which Jesus died and left in lowercase for the cross of one's own home or parish.

Foolish and unfaithful men needed you in order to inflict their cruelty upon the Gentlest of Man, but that is not why we celebrate you—rather, it is for the wisest love of Him Who freely embraced you. For these men were unable to accomplish anything unless He in His wisdom allowed it; nor could He undergo anything unless He in His mercy willed it. Those men chose you to carry out their most faithless crime, but He chose you to bring to completion the work of His faithfulness. Those men used you to betray a just man over to death, but because of you, He rescued sinners from death.

They used you to destroy life; He used you to annihilate death. They used you to condemn the Savior; He used you to save the condemned. They tried to bring the Living One to death; He used you to vivify the dead. They were foolish and cruel; He was wise and merciful. Therefore, oh admirable cross, we hold you in esteem not for the cruel stupidity for which these men wanted to exploit you but rather for the mercy and wisdom you brought about.

How, then, shall I praise you; in what way shall I exalt you? With what affection should I pray to you, and with what amount of joy shall I glorify in you?

Through you, hell was destroyed and damned up for all those who have been redeemed. Through you, the evil spirits tremble—they are held down, defeated, and stomped upon. Through you, the world is renewed and is now decorated in the truth that gleams and the justice that reigns. Through you, sinful human nature is now justified, the damned have been saved, any slave to sin and to the underworld is now freed, and the dead have been brought back to life. On account of you that blessed city in heaven has been restored and is made complete. Through you—for our sake, God—the Son of God was obedient to the Father, even to the point of death (cf. Phil 2:8), which is why He is now exalted and has received the name above every other name (cf. Phil 2:9). Because of you, He has prepared His throne and has begun His reign.

Oh cross, you who were chosen and set aside for such overwhelming benefits, neither the intellect nor the words of either angels or humans could ever sufficiently praise and exalt the work completed on you. Oh you, on whom and through whom is my salvation and my life; Oh you, on whom and through whom is my entire and only good, "may I never boast except" in you (Gal 6:14). Why would I have been conceived, born, and lived, why would I enjoy all the goods of this life, if I am only to descend into hell afterwards? Would it not have been better for me if I had never been conceived (see Mt 26:24)? And this would certainly be the case if I had not been redeemed by you.

With what kind of feeling am I to glory in you, for without you there would be nothing to glory in, but for all eternity the sorrow and miseries of hell would have mastery over me? With what sweetness am I to rejoice in you, through whom that slavishness of hell which I have inherited, has been given over to the kingdom of heaven? With what joy am I to be grateful to you, without whom the future would horrify me—if even for only a moment—but through whom I now expect to rejoice forever? For even though I now serve God between hope and fear, I am certain that I shall come to all those good things of heaven through you if I only give thanks, love, and live glorifying in you.

Therefore, allow my glory to be through you and in you. Allow my true hope to be through you and in you. For through you, my sins are absolved, and through you, my soul died to the old (cf. Eph 4:22) and was reborn to a new life of righteousness. I plead that through baptism, you wash me from all my sins in which I have been conceived and in which I have been born (cf. Ps 51:5) and cleanse me again from all the sins I have committed since I have been reborn so that through you, I may come to all those delights for which the human person has been created, through the same Jesus Christ our Lord Who is blessed forever. Amen.

Questions for Prayerful Reflection

- Take some time to sit or kneel before your favorite crucifix or icon of Mount Calvary. Gain some quiet, and then ask Jesus on the Cross: "What have I done for You? What am I doing for You? What shall I do for You?" Simply sit with those questions, perhaps reviewing your past, looking at your current life, and anticipating your future. What feelings surface? What sins are still to be confessed? What new plan or resolve is Jesus asking of you?

- What are the crosses in your life right now? Can you name them and then pray to unite them to the Cross of Jesus, where He can transform any death, disappointment, or failing into something unexpectedly new and beautiful?
- What are the "delights" for which you have been created? Although we live in a fallen world, do you allow yourself to enjoy the things God gives you, and do you treat those pleasures as gifts of the Almighty? Be specific.

II.

Prayers with Mother Mary

Prayer to Saint Mary When the Mind Is Weighed Down by Acedia

Devout Christians who pray to a saint understand that the saint is not the source of their answered prayer but a prayer partner with those on earth who petition and adore God. Praying is like singing in that, first, we can do it alone, but it usually sounds better when accomplished in harmony with others. Too, when a music teacher instructs, "Sing to the melody," one sings "with" the melody—in tune with what is being played. That is how the Church prays. Although there is a long-standing tradition of our "praying to the saints," we are, in fact, praying alongside and with our saints, even Mother Mary, all harmoniously adoring and petitioning God, as the saints do nothing and have no authority apart from the power of the Almighty.

This is the first of three prayers Anselm offers alongside Mother Mary's sinless prayers to the Holy Trinity. This first (number five in Anselm's entire collection) is offered when one feels the effects of the deadly sin of spiritual sloth or acedia (from the Greek meaning "not to care"). While the first three deadly sins of pride, envy, and wrath are familiarly called "the cold sins" and the last three of avarice, gluttony, and lust are "the warm sins," right in the middle is acedia, the sin of being lukewarm and not really caring about anything essential. Such sloth is not to be equated with physical laziness but is more of a spiritual malaise, an uncaring about anything important, with the effect of the soul suffering from acedia taking on too many projects, spreading itself out too thinly among pursuits or pastimes that do not really matter. Thomas Aquinas calls this sin "the tendency to wander" (Summa Theologiae II-II 35.4), while Anselm sees it as a vice which is monstrous (immanitate) because, without any sense of priorities, the slothful soul will settle for anything that comes its way, flitting about anything that happens to capture its fancy.

Holy one—and after God, the holiest among all—Holy Mary, my mother of commendable virginity and virgin with loving fruitfulness, you are she who brought forth the Son of the Most High God, who gave birth to the Savior of the condemned human race. My Lady, most refulgent with such holiness, supereminent in such dignity, it is certain that you are not less endowed than anyone else in power and in piety. So, oh mother of Life, mother of Salvation, temple of right religion and mercy, I am trying to present my miserable soul to you, anemic with the diseases of all my sins, a soul torn apart by the wounds of its misdeeds and putrid with the ulcers of immodesty.

I rely on you, as I am near death, asking that through your sovereign merits and your pious prayers, you will deign to make me whole. For a monstrous stupor separates us, loving lady, so that I hardly have a sense of my abnormal lethargy. My sickness is so disgusting, sordid, and foul-smelling that it fears that you might turn your merciful gaze away from it. That is why it looks to you for conversion, but despair holds me back such that even my mouth becomes mute when it goes to pray.

Oh my sins, my iniquities, if your poison has put my soul to sleep, why do you make it even more horrendous with your filth, with the result that even mercy is unable to turn its face toward it?[13] If your dullness is so great that there is no hope of my being heard, why does shame still silence my voice when I go to pray? If you have arranged my mind so it now loves you, why do you force my mind's senses into an unfeeling indifference? Oh, how shameful is the sordidness of sin when it appears before the brilliance of holiness! What confusion an unclean conscience experiences when it comes before the face of refulgent purity!

Oh, you are blessed among all women, a woman who surpasses even the angels in innocence, surpassing the saints in piety. My spirit is gasping with death and longs to be recognized by your kindness, but it blushes when such brilliances gazes upon it.

---

13 Throughout this prayer, Anselm moves from talking to Mary to talking directly toward his sins. Notice the sins he has mentioned so far: they begin with the consequences of the vice of acedia—an anemic soul, spiritual stupor and lethargy, and such indifference is what allows the more "sordid and foul-smelling" sins to occur. Or, as the old adage puts it, in taking such inventory of his soul, Anselm not only names his sins aloud which is never easy to do (why the sacrament of Reconciliation can be so intimidating but so healing at the same time), he also shows how true accountability can finally take place for those longing to grow in holiness.

I therefore long to ask you, lady, that by a mere glimpse of your mercy, you might cure the plague and ulcers of my sins, but I remain conquered by their stench and sordidness. I shudder in fear, lady, to reveal to you my horrid and infected self, fearing that you might become horrified of me because of them, and I am not able to be seen without these. Oh, how wretched I am!

How disturbed and confused is the reality of sin. Indeed you, my sins, how you madden my heart by tearing it apart, how you corrode it with distractions and how you torture it with lack of care.[14]

---

[14] The mystery of iniquity is a long-standing problem in Christian anthropology, as St. Paul knew so well: "For I do not do what I want, but I do what I hate" (Rom 7:15b). One of the tactics of the enemy of our human nature is to make sin look attractive and satisfying, and it might be, but only for a fleeting moment. This is what causes the maddening torture and confusion Anselm here describes, and which we all know. St. John Paul also included Mother Mary in the work of reconciling sinners to God: "I likewise invite you to turn with me to the immaculate heart of Mary, mother of Jesus, in whom is effected the reconciliation of God with humanity . . . , is accomplished the work of reconciliation, because she has received from God the fullness of grace in virtue of the redemptive sacrifice of Christ. Truly Mary has been associated with God, by virtue of her divine motherhood, in the work of reconciliation" (*Reconciliation and Penance* §35).

For these sins of mine, oh lady, desire to be known by you so they can be cured, but they flee from you so as not to be cursed. Yet without confession they cannot be cured, but they cannot be divulged without confusion. If they are hidden, they remain uncurable; if they are seen, they are detestable. They burn me with pain and shake me with fear. They overwhelm me with their heaviness, they weigh me down with their size, and they defeat me with their shame.

Oh you, that powerful in piety and pious in power, Maria, from whom arose that Font of Mercy, I pray that you do not refuse me true mercy. For you know well where such true mercy is to be found. Before the brilliance of your holiness, I am confused by the obscenity of my iniquity, but surely, lady, you will not be embarrassed to show such a wretch your inherent tenderness? If I confess my sinfulness, surely you would not withhold your kindness? If my wretchedness is too great to be absolved, will your mercy not be less than what it should be? Oh lady, how greatly sordid are my sins in the sight of God and before you; how much greater then must His protection and your help be!

Heal then, most clement Mary, my infirmity and wipe away this stained soul that surely offends you. Take away, most kind Mary, my indifference and do not feel the filth that must horrify you. Most loving lady, ensure that this does not sadden you and that there is no sullying of your sincerity. Lady, hear me and heal the soul of this sinner, your servant. My lady, do this by the power of the fruit of your womb, Who is seated at the right hand of the Omnipotent Father, praiseworthy and glorious over all forever. Amen.

Questions for Prayerful Reflection

- How would you describe your relationship with Mary? Is she more symbolic or is she a real, living mother who plays a pivotal role in your life with Christ her Son? How do you rely on Mary?
- Do you suffer from the sin of sloth? Do you find it hard to concentrate, to focus, to give yourself entirely over to that which is worthwhile? This may be an indication that you have come unmoored from what is truly important and find it easier to commit only half-heartedly and without

any zeal. Can you ask Mary to pray for you, the Mother of God who fostered the ability to ponder all things in her heart (Lk 2:19)?

- How does your spiritual life change when you think of Mary being intimately involved in how you see yourself, how you interact with her Son, and how you look out upon the world? Does having a mother, a sister, or a woman friend affect your soul at all? Does remembering that Jesus chose to be part of a family affect how you might look at your own?

Holy Prayer to Mary When the Mind Is Anxious with Fear

The second prayer "to" Mary (the sixth overall) captures Anselm's obvious struggle with fear. Being anxious with fear (sollicita cum timore), as he put it, is an ancient and perennial reality. Fear is not always a sin, as it can be an immaculate moment of wonder, as Mary experienced when she learned of her role in saving the world (Lk 1:30), what the Church Fathers called "chaste" or "filial fear."

But "servile fear" is the result of the Fall and humanity's unwillingness to trust completely in God's goodness. In this prayer (number six in Anselm's collection), we are to ask Our Lady to help buttress our courage in living this life, fraught with inevitable disappointments and betrayals. We meet Mary when she is contending with angels and leave her as she has fought her way through the madding crowd, defied the Roman soldiers, and seeks to console her dying Son on the Cross—truly a model of Christian courage!

Virgin venerated around the world, loving mother of the human race, a woman marveled by the angels, most holy Mary, by whose blessed virginity has made all chastity sacred, and whose glorious childbearing has made all fruitfulness salvific! Great lady, to whom the joyous gathering of the just give thanks, and in whom the fearful band of the condemned take refuge: I, a terribly anxious sinner, find protection in you, mighty and merciful lady.

It already seems, lady, that I am before the omnipotent justice of the stern Judge, and am considering the unbearable intensity of His wrath, while the enormity of my sins dangles over me, the immensity of their punishments being imminent. Therefore, lady most clement, as I am quaking with horror and am shaken with fear, is there a more reliable intercession upon which I could call upon but yours, whose womb nurtured the world's reconciliation?

Where else could I so securely hope in such a swift support than from you whom I know brought forth the world's atonement? Or, whose intercession is able to more easily secure pardon for the guilty than she who breastfed the Just One Who punishes or mercifully forgives all and each one of us? Most blessed one, it is thus impossible that you could ever forget those merits which are unique to you but necessary for us—so, most gentle mother, it is actually unbelievable that you could ever fail to have mercy on us miserable sinners who call out to you.

Well does the world realize, and in no way do we sinners try to conceal this from the world: it is enough that I proclaim it and it is enough that we know, my lady, who is the "Son of Man" or to whom the Son of Man comes to bring the salvation they had forfeited. Now you, my lady, the mother of my hope, would you ever be so disgusted with me that you would forget the One you so mercifully bore into the world, so joyfully brought forth, and so lovingly held?

That Son of Man came into the world to save the lost by His own accord (see Lk 19:10); how then could the Mother of God ever refuse to cure the lost who call out to her? That good Son of Man came to call sinners to repentance (Mk 1:15), so how could the Mother of God ever spurn anyone who prays in repentance? That one, I say, the Good God, the Gentle Man, the Merciful Son of God, the Dutiful Son of Man, came to search out the errant sinner, and you, His good mother, powerful Mother of God, would you ever turn back a miserable sinner who prays to you?

For behold, oh human virgin from whom God is born a man so that sinful man might be saved: behold before your Good Son and before His good mother is a sinful man who repents and confesses, who groans and prays. I thus ask both of you, good Lord and good lady, I beseech you, devout Son and devout mother, through this truth—which is the only hope of sinners—that you truly be her Son and you truly be His mother so that the sinner may be saved. Allow, then, this sinner to be absolved, cared for, cleansed, and saved. In so doing, he proves who he is: proving he is a sinner who belongs to you because he knows you two are both Son and mother for the salvation of sinners. And, indeed, I am that sinner who is held by you both.

For when I sin against the Son, I have bereaved His mother, and I cannot offend the mother without doing injury to her Son.[15] What will you do, then, you sinner? To where will you flee, sinful man? Who will reconcile me to the Son if His mother is hostile toward me? Or with the Son angered, who will placate His mother for me? But even if I have offended you both equally, are you both not still merciful? The guilty man thus flees from a just God to the loving mother of that merciful God. That guilty party then takes refuge from the offended mother in the loving Son of that kindly mother. The accused is thus transferred from one to the other and hurls himself between the loving Son and the loving mother.

---

[15] Here Anselm's teaching is reflected in St. John Paul's beautiful insight: "I was already convinced that Mary leads us to Christ, but at that time I began to realize also that Christ leads us to His Mother" (*Gift and Mystery*, p. 29). This exchange is suggested in John's Gospel as well, in that the final words of Mary are recorded there at Cana: "Do whatever He tells you" (Jn 2:5), while among Jesus's last words were spoken for all: "Then he said to the disciple, 'Behold, your mother.' And from that hour the disciple took her into his home" (Jn 19:27). Mary's entire purpose was to point us to Jesus, and among His last gifts to His disciples was the presence of His mother.

Loving Lord, spare the servant of your mother. Loving lady, spare the servant of your Son. Good Son, make peace with Your mother for the sake of your servant. Good mother, reconcile your servant with your Son. When I hurl myself between these two immense loves, I will not fall into two competing powers: Good Son, good mother, let this truth I confess about you two never be in vain. Let me never be embarrassed over what I hope about the love that is found in you. I love the truth which I now confess about you, and I plead to you for the love which I hope to know in you.

Tell me, Judge of the world, whom do You spare, Reconciler of the world, whom do You reconcile if You, Lord, damn—and you, lady, withhold—your common goodness and love from this insignificant man who now confesses his evil deeds with such heartache? Savior of each, tell me whom you shall save. Mother of salvation, tell me for whom you will pray. With You, Lord, leading the way, and with you, lady, consenting, the agonies which vex this self-accused sinner call out to you. If hell consumes this sinner who knows he is guilty, he still prays to you. If the entire underworld devours this poor wretch who is in despair, he still hopes in you.

God, Who was made the Son of a woman for the sake of mercy; woman, who was made the Mother of God on account of that same mercy, have mercy on the merciless, You, Lord, by forgiving and you, Lady, by interceding. Or, may you both reveal to the exile where he can most securely find mercy, and show him in whose sovereignty he can most surely confide.

For *if*—or, better, *because*—my iniquity is so great and my faith so meager, because my love is so lukewarm, my prayer so pathetic, and my desire to atone so imperfect, I deserve neither the forgiveness of my sins nor the grace of salvation. This is why I beg you: however meager you may see my merits to be, let your mercies not prove to be lacking.

This is why I pray, praying that you hear me because of who you are and not because of who I am, and that due to the love which you pour out and through the power in which you abound, that I may be kept away from the deserved punishments of the damned and instead enter into the joys of the saints, so I might praise You, God, Who is blessed and exalted for ever and ever. Amen.

Questions for Prayerful Reflection

- What is it you most fear? Is it the loss of a loved one, loss of financial security, or a job, perhaps you fear your own death and judgment above all?
- Is there a particular person whom you have always held out as courageous? What was it about that person that bolstered your own confidence? Is there a scene in Mary's life which reminds you of this?
- What could you ask Mary to assist you with? How could you best call upon her maternal care and strength today?

Prayer to Mary Asking Her for Her Love and for the Love of Christ

The third prayer to Mary (number seven in Anselm's collection) reminds us that charity is the only real virtue that endures forever, the act of the will which consecrates all our actions, and itself the only act for which we shall be judged. Anselm realizes how charity is not simply one virtue among many but the one grace that will transform every other aspect of his life.

This lengthy prayer begins by seeing Mary among the other women with the same name, singling out Mary the Mother of God as man's surest refuge. We then hear Anselm honor Mary by extolling her virtues and pleading for a share in her immaculate love of God. Here is invoked as Queen, as a grand lady, as the Advocatrix of the human race, and the Mother of all humanity.

Mary, you great Mary, most blessed of all the Marys, you who are the greatest among all women, great lady and worthy of praise, let my heart love you and my mouth declare your praise. May my mind desire to venerate you, and may my soul long to pray to you, because my entire being now commends itself to you as my surest refuge.

Strive, my soul's inmost being, strive as much as you can—if you are able to do anything—to arouse all that which is in me to praise Mary's merits, to love her joy, to admire her heavenly state, and to beg her kindness. For you stand in daily need of her protection, and in such need you should desire her by needing her, implore her by needing her, pray to her by imploring her, and if all of this does not resonate with what you really want, at least let your desires transcend, or even go against, what you actually deserve.

Queen of angels, matron of the world, mother of Him Who cleanses the world, I confess that my heart is too unclean, so that it is justifiably too embarrassed to address one so flawless, nor can it worthily reach one so spotless just by addressing her. You, mother of my heart's illumination, you who are the nursemaid of my mind's salvation, my entire heart begs you as much as it is able. Hear me, lady, and be favorable toward me, my most powerful advocatrix,[16] that the sins of my mind be washed away, that my darkness be illumined, that my lukewarm heart become fire, and my listlessness be awoken. Your blessed holiness is above all others, behind only your Son—but through your omnipotent and glorious Son, your holiness is exalted by Him.

---

[16] Vatican II puts this truth as such: "The Blessed Virgin's salutary influence on men originates not in any inner necessity but in the disposition of God. It flows forth from the superabundance of the merits of Christ, rests on his mediation, depends entirely on it and draws all its power from it. It does not hinder in any way the immediate union of the faithful with Christ but, on the contrary, fosters it" (*Lumen Gentium* §60).

And since you are above all and after only the Lord, my God and my all, Who is your Son, my heart knows you and venerates you. My heart loves you and begs you for your affection, not because I am imperfect in what I long for, but because it is your Son Who creates and saves, redeems and renews. Mother of the life of my soul, nourisher of my soul's Redeemer, you who nursed the Savior of my entire existence!

What shall I say? My tongue fails because my mind is inadequate. Lady, oh lady, my entire being is attentive to how it owes you gratitude for all your gifts. But my mind has no worthy thoughts, and it shames me to offer you anything unworthy of you. So, what could I ever worthily say to the mother of my Creator and Savior, through whose holiness my sins have been forgiven, through whose virginity incorruptibility is granted to me, and through whose purity my soul falls in love with the Lord and is thus espoused to its God?

How could I ever communicate anything worthwhile about the mother of my God and my Lord, by whose fruitfulness I have been set free from captivity, whose childbearing has saved me from eternal death, and by whose Son I have been brought back from exile in misery and hence returned to my homeland of blessedness?

Blessed among women (cf. Lk 1:42a), all these graces were bestowed upon me by "the blessed fruit of thy womb" (Lk 1:42b) in the regeneration of His baptism—some still in hope, some even now.[17] However, I rejected all of these gifts through sinning, and consequently, I can barely hope at all and actually have nothing. What then? If these gifts vanished because of my faults, could I ever become ungrateful towards her through whom all these good things freely came to me?

Stop, lest I pile blasphemy upon blasphemy. I am immensely grateful for what I have had, yet I am saddened over what I no longer have, praying that I might have it again. I am certain that because through her Son I have been able to receive grace, I am able to receive it again through the merits of His mother.

Accordingly, lady, life's port and door of salvation, you who are the way of reconciliation and the access to restoration, I beg you through your fruitfulness which brought about our Savior, ensure my sins be

---

[17] Although a constant throughout the entire Christian story, Anselm may be picking up on a constant theme in Augustine and how the ancient bishop casts the gifts of Christianity as things we enjoy now but not fully, employing a clever wordplay: we live the Christian life now in hope (*in spe*) but not yet in its full reality (*in re*). (See *Homilies on the Gospel of John*, 124.5.)

absolved and the grace to live a holy life be granted, and even until the end of my days keep me, your servant, under your protection.

You are the fortress of universal reparation, the cause of human reconciliation, vessel and temple of life and of worldwide salvation. I have not appreciated your merits enough, and in one so small like myself, it is even worse to downplay your kindnesses, especially as the world lovingly rejoices in you, and in rejoicing in you, it cries out all that you are.

For you, most admirable lady, are known for your singular virginity, venerated for an unmatchable holiness. You show the world its Lord and its God, Whom it had not known. You present to the world its Creator now visible Whom before you it was not able to see. You bring forth the world's Redeemer, for Whom this lost world hungers. To this guilty world, you bore its Reconciler, Whom it did not have before. Through your fruitfulness, my matron, the sinful world is justified, the damned are saved, the expelled are brought back.

Lady, your Son redeemed this captive world, He made the diseased whole, and He resurrected the dead! So, while the world had been enveloped in darkness, trapped and oppressed by the demons under whose power it was laid flat, it is now illuminated by the sun arising from you, which snapped their snares and trampled upon their dominion.

Heaven, stars, earth, rivers, day, night, and whatever else is under the power or use of humanity are fallen (Rom 8:19–23), but now they give thanks for having been stripped of that sort of grandeur, lady. For through you, they have been renewed and have been granted a new sort of ineffable grace.[18] For when they lost their innate dignity in the dominion of God and had been stripped of their habit of praising Him—for which they had been made—it was as if all things were dead.

---

[18] Anselm sees how even brute creation is renewed by Mary's "yes." St. Paul knows that "all creation is groaning in labor pains even until now" (Rom 8:22), and the Old Testament authors saw how all creation proclaims God's glory (cf. Ps 148; Dn 3). Most of the early Church likewise commented on this creaturely kaleidoscope of natural praise; for example: "The angels, likewise, all pray; every creature prays; cattle and wild beasts pray and bend their knees; and when they issue from their layers and lairs, they look up heavenward with no idle mouth, making their breath vibrate after their own manner. Nay, the birds too, rising out of the nest, upraise themselves heavenward, and, instead of hands, expand the cross of their wings, and say somewhat to seem like prayer." Tertullian, *On Prayer* §29.

All creatures were overwhelmed with oppression and had lost their splendor, now being in the service of enslaving idols for which they were never created. But now they have truly been renewed by rightly offering praise, now being ruled by those who confess God and are thus glorified in this very service. Now all of creation is exulted with a new and inestimable grace, for all creatures now recognize God Himself, their very Creator, not only as He invisibly reigns over them but also visibly as He sanctifies them in His service. All these good things have come into the world because of the blessed fruit of Mary's womb.

But, Mary, why do I only discourse about all your gifts which fill this world? They have descended into the underworld and have risen to the heavens. Through the fullness of your grace, all those in hell can now be delivered and thus know happiness, and those above in heaven, in fact, rejoice at their restoration. By the glorious Son of your glorious virginity, all the just who died before He came into this world are now exultant in praise because their captivity has been removed, and the angels are grateful in the restoration of their once crumbling city.[19]

[19] Anselm here may have in mind an ancient Holy Saturday

Oh, you are the singularly admirable woman, a woman admirably unique, through whom the worldly elements have been renewed, hell has been redeemed, demons are trampled underfoot, men are saved, and angels are reincorporated to their rightful place.[20] Oh woman full and lavishly full of grace, with whose abundance every creature is sprinkled and has been made green again!

Homily (c. third or fourth century?) in which our anonymous preacher describes how Christ descends into Sheol, "to seek out our first parent like a lost sheep; he wishes to visit those who sit in darkness and in the shadow of death. He goes to free the prisoner Adam and his fellow-prisoner Eve from their pains, he who is God, and Adam's son. The Lord goes in to them holding his victorious weapon, his cross. When Adam, the first created man, sees him, he strikes his breast in terror and calls out to all: 'My Lord be with you all.' And Christ in reply says to Adam: 'And with your spirit.' And grasping his hand he raises him up, saying: 'Awake, O sleeper, and arise from the dead, and Christ shall give you light.'" Accessed at https://www.vatican.va/spirit/documents/spirit_20010414_omelia-sabato-santo_en.html.

[20] Here Anselm is most likely continuing St. Augustine's belief that the number of fallen angels will be replaced by the elect. This claim is made out of the fittingness that the heavenly Jerusalem enjoy the number of saints God intended and when some angels chose to leave the City of God, God chose to replace them and even—so surmises Augustine—increase that number exponentially (see *Enchiridion on Faith, Hope, and Love*, 9.29).

Oh, blessed and superabundantly blessed, through whose blessings all nature is blessed, and it is not only the creature that is blessed by the Creator but even the Creator is blessed by the creature. Oh, highly dignified lady whom the affections of my soul try to follow, how do you elude even the keenness of my mind? You, who are so beautiful to bring to mind and so loving to contemplate, so sweet to love—how do you escape the vastness of my heart?

Lady, please wait for the staggering soul who follows you. Do not hide from him, lady, but see the weakness of the soul who seeks you. Have mercy, lady, on the soul who gasps for you longingly.

Mary is a marvel, and I contemplate her at a sublime height. There is no equal to Mary; nothing and no one except God is greater than Mary. God offered His Son, Who alone from His own heart is brought forth equally to Him, loved as His own Self, and to Mary, He gave His Son, and from Mary came forth her Son—not another, but the Same Son, so that in the order of nature there is only One Son of both, Son of God and Son of Mary.[21]

---

[21] Here crucial lines of the Nicene Creed echo: "I believe in one Lord Jesus Christ, the Only Begotten Son of God, born of the

All nature is created by God and God is born of Mary: God created all things and Mary brought forth God. God Who created all things, also made Himself from Mary and in so doing, recreated all things which He had created. God is able to bring all things out of nothing (Heb 11:3; Rom 4:17; Ps 33:6–9; Wis 1:14), but would not recreate it unwillingly, so He first made Himself the Son of Mary.[22]

God is therefore the Father of all created things, and Mary is the mother of all recreated things. God is the Father of all that has been established, and Mary is the mother of all that has been reestablished. God brought forth His Son through Whom all things have been made (Jn 1:3), and Mary brought forth her Son through Whom all things are saved. God brought

---

Father before all ages. God from God, Light from Light, true God from true God, begotten, not made, consubstantial with the Father; through him all things were made. For us men and for our salvation he came down from heaven, and by the Holy Spirit was incarnate of the Virgin Mary, and became man."

[22] For more on creation out of nothing (*ex nihil*), see the *Catechism of the Catholic Church* §297. Regarding Anselm's insistence that God had to create without permission but refuses to save a free-willed creature without his or her free assent, recall Augustine's great insight that "God had to make you without you . . . but he won't justify you without you" (*Sermon* 169.13).

forth His Son without Whom absolutely nothing would exist, and Mary brought forth her Son without Whom absolutely nothing would exist well.

Oh truly, "the Lord is with you" (Mt 28:18–20), for you are the one to whom the Lord gave over His own self so that all the nature which is in you might also be with Him. Mary, I ask you, through the grace by which the Lord is one with you and which He wanted to be one with you, in the same way and by means of the same grace, let your mercy always be with me, let your love always be with me, and let your care for me always be with you. As long as it needs, let the clamor of my needs be with you, and as long as I need, let the kindliness of your love always be with me. May the good wishes of your blessedness always be with me, and may your compassion for my misery, as much as it needs, always be with you.

Oh, blessed woman, everything that is adverse to you and anything that is against you is necessarily lost. Likewise, whatever turns toward you and is seen by you is never going to perish. For just as God brought forth Him in whom all things live so, lady—oh, flower of virginity—you brought Him forth, the

One through Whom all that is dead is brought back to life. And as God saves the blessed angels from sin through His Son, so you—ornament of purity, save miserable men from their sinning through your Son.

Just as the Son of God is the joy of the just, you are the security of the fruitful, and your Son is the reconciliation of sinners. For there would be no reconciliation had you not chastely conceived Him, no justification had you not wholly cherished Him in your womb, no salvation had you not virginally brought Him forth. Therefore, oh lady, you are the mother of both the Justifier as well as those justified, the bearer of the Reconciler as well as those reconciled, mother of the Savior as well as the saved.

Oh, blessed security, you who are my safe refuge—Mother of God and our mother. His mother in Whom alone we hope and the only One we are to fear (cf. Mt 10:28) is also our mother. So, mother, let me acknowledge: the mother of Him Who alone saves and Who alone can also damn is also our mother.

But you are blessed and exalted not only for yourself but also for us. Ah, but what I behold! I see something so great and so loving coming to us through you, something which I rejoice when seeing and which I dare not describe when rejoicing. Lady, if you are His mother, are we not also your sons and daughters, His brothers and sisters? But who are those brothers and sisters, and to whom do they belong? Should I answer this from the rejoicing of my heart, or should I just stay silent lest my mouth be overwhelmed with too much jubilation? But since I confess this in loving you, why should I not confess you by praising you? Then I shall speak not out of any pride but only out of gratitude.

Through the restoration of our lives, He made us sons and daughters of His own mother by being born of a mother and thus becoming a partaker of our human nature (see Col 2:9; Heb 2:14). He thus bids us to confess that we are His brothers and sisters. He is both our Judge and our Brother, our Savior and our Brother, and finally—because of you, Mary—our God has become our Brother. With what certitude ought we hope and with what consolation! Why should we ever allow ourselves to fear, since our salvation or our condemnation depends on the judgment of a good Brother and a loving mother?

With what affection are we supposed to love this Brother and this mother? With what familiarity do we commit ourselves to them? By what security are we to flee to them? With what agreeableness are we to take refuge in them? No doubt our good Brother forgives us when we go astray, shunning what our sins in fact deserve. No doubt He Himself will give us the penance we seek.

Our mother prays and intercedes for us; she appeals and urges Him on our behalf, asking her Son to be well-disposed toward us. She begs her Son for her sons and daughters, the naturally-born One for her adopted ones, the Lord for the servants. May the good Son hear His Mother for the sake of His brothers and sisters, the Only-Begotten for those she has adopted, the Lord for captives freed.

Mary, how much we owe you! Lady, Mother, through whom we have such a Brother, with what thanks and with what praise could we ever repay you? Great Lord, you are our greater Brother; great lady, you are our better mother: teach my heart with what reverence it should have when contemplating you two. You, Lord, are good, and you, lady, are good; you both are so tender, speak and teach my soul how to recall you in love and how to rejoice in you, rejoicing in tenderness and so be touched by pleasing you. Strike my soul and ignite it with your love. Let my heart sigh continuously with your love, melt my soul and forget my flesh.

Oh, if only my innermost soul would burn with the tender fervor of your love so that my fleshy self would shrivel away. Would that the inmost spirit of my soul be so affected by the sweetness of your affections, that the marrow of my body would dry up![23]

Lord—Son of my lady—and lady—mother of my Lord—if I am not worthy to be blessed by your love, certainly you are not unworthy to be loved. In fact, you both should be loved more. Therefore, most tender Lord and lady, do not begrudge what I am asking you, even though I do admit that I am unworthy in asking it: I pray that you grant to this

---

[23] Christians must remember that Paul most usually speaks of the "flesh" not literally but as synonymous with "the world," with what keeps us away from God's self. Such a use of "flesh" or "body" is, for Paul, always contrasted with the things of "the spirit," but this must never mean that the body is inherently bad. For what Christian, following a God made flesh, could ever reconcile a hostile view of the human body with the entire point of the Son of God's becoming man? What Paul is saying is that the "old man," the "fleshy man," the "sinful man" must die so one is able to surrender wholly—body and soul—to the indwelling and the promptings of the Holy Spirit.

supplicant soul—not according to my merit but on account of yours—give to me whatever is worthy of your love. While wholly unworthy, I ask that you give me that which I can return to you, which is worthy of you. But if you do not want to grant what I desire to have, at least do not deprive me what it is I owe you.

Maybe I am speaking to you presumptuously, but your goodness instills confidence in me. Yet I speak to my Lord and to my lady, "even though I am dust and ashes" (Gn 18:27).[24] Lord and lady: is it not much greater when you give grace to a beggar who asks and in no way deserves it rather than for you to exact from one what he justly owes? For the first is mercy worth praising, while the other is an injustice worth condemning.[25] Dispense your grace then, you

---

[24] As Anselm does so often, being very aware of his unworthiness, Abraham refers to himself as only "dust and ashes" as he interacts with God, interceding for the people of Sodom.

[25] Anselm's satisfaction theory is in obvious play here: granting grace to a destitute beggar is clearly mercy but making him pay for what he never could would be an injustice. This is why God Himself must become a man in order to redeem what no child of Adam could ever afford.

most loving pair, so that you may receive what is owed to you.

It is both desirable and becoming that you show me your mercy. For acting unjustly towards you is desirable for no one and unbecoming for all. I pray that you be merciful to me so that I never dishonor you and thus become cursed. Kind Lord and kind lady, please see that my reaching out to you is not difficult, but grant your love to my soul, which does not seek you unjustly and which you justly command. For I do not want to be ungrateful for all your kindnesses because that is justly horrifying and something which you would not unjustly punish.

Certainly, Jesus, Son of God, and you, Mary, His mother, you both desire what is just, and that whatever is loved by you should be loved by us as well. Therefore, Good Son, I ask that through the very same love with which You love your mother, and that as You really love her and want to be loved by her, grant unto me that I too may really love her. Good mother, I ask that through the love you have for your Son, that as you really love Him and want to be loved by Him, grant unto me that I too may really love Him.

For I am begging for that which You must truly desire. Why does He not treat me as my sins deserve when it is in His power to do so? Lover and Mercy of mankind, can You still love those who have condemned You to death? Are You actually capable of turning away from those who call out to both Your love as well as to Your mother? Dear Mother of our Lover—you, who carried Him in your womb and who was found worthy to nurse Him, are you unable, or are you not willing, to bestow His and your love on those who call out to you?

Because of all this, I venerate both of you insofar as my mind is worthy. As far as my heart is up to the task, it loves you both. As far as my soul can, it chooses both of you. As far as my flesh is able, it stands in service of you both, and in this is let my life come to completion, so that for all eternity my entire being may sing this Psalm: "Blessed be the Lord forever, let it be so, let it be so" (Ps 89:53).

Questions for Prayerful Reflection

- At the beginning of this prayer, Anselm focuses on Mary's joy and her kindness.

Do you see those as particularly maternal or feminine traits? How would you define true joy (as opposed to mere happiness), and what do you mean by kindness? Where do you practice these Marian qualities, and how could you grow more joyful and even kinder throughout your busy day?

- Does your relationship with Mary always bring you back to her Son Jesus? Too, does your time with Jesus always lead you to His mother Mary? What do you need to understand this interrelationship better, and how might it affect your prayer life or even deeper understanding of the Faith?
- A major part of this prayer is creation's role in our salvation. Paul tells us that all created things should speak to us of the invisible God (Rom 1:19–20), and Mary has always been Queen of heaven and earth. How does the world of creation help (or hinder) your prayer? Do you "find" God more easily outside or inside? Has your appreciation of nature in this

regard been marred by wrong-headed calls for environmentalism? Do remember that God is the Creator of every animal, flower, and creature, and in them one can learn about the One Who delights in them as an Artist in His works.

III.

Prayers through the Church Triumphant

The Council of Ephesus in AD 431 distinguished between the worship owed to God alone (latria) and the veneration we all owe the saints (dulia). Yet in this distinction arose another level of heavenly honor—hyperdulia—a special veneration owed to Mary for her unique and unmatchable role in humanity's salvation. The following prayers are then to be offered through those saints who would also venerate Mary in a special way. We have included prayers here for John the Baptist, Mary Magdalene, St. Peter, two to John the Evangelist, St. Stephen, St. Paul, and the founder of the Benedictines to which Anselm belonged, St. Benedict.

Prayer to John the Baptist

Number eight in Anselm's collection of prayers is this singular offering to John the Baptist. This prayer begins by looking at the one who, after Mary, first recognizes the lordship of Jesus Christ! This primacy is then contrasted with Adam and his first act of being unaware of God's real presence. This dissimilarity is used by Anselm to teach that the one Who stands at the head of creation and the Old Testament is now giving way to the one Who marks the beginning of the New Covenant, heralding God's glorious Second Creation in Christ.

After Mary, John the Baptist was the most revered saint in the early Church and well into the Middle Ages. In fact, apart from Mary's (September 8) and, of course, Christ at Christmas (December 25), John's natural birthday, June 24, is the only other birthday the Church celebrates liturgically (a birth symbolically set at the midsummer when the days begin to shorten because John himself declared, "He must increase; I must decrease," in Jn 3:30). For it was fairly common among the Church Fathers as well as the medieval Doctors that while John the Baptist was not conceived immaculately, he was cleansed from original sin upon leaping in the presence of the unborn Christ. So, while all other saints are celebrated on the day of their death, their heavenly birthday, as an assurance that the life they had led was worthy of emulation, John's birth guaranteed a holy life because of his encounter with Christ while still in the womb.

Saint John, you are that John who baptized God, the John who was praised by an archangel before you were brought forth from your father Zaccariah (Lk 1:12–19) and filled with God even before you were born from your mother (Lk 1:41). And you, you recognized God even before you knew anything about the world! Even before your mother carried you in her womb and would eventually show you the light of day, you pointed out to your pregnant mother the pregnant mother of God. You are the John about whom the Lord said: "Among those born of women there has been none greater" (Mt 11:11) and here before you, good sir—so great, so holy, so blessed—comes a wicked worm, a grieving little man who can barely feel grief and who is dead in the soul, a sinner who can't even find pity for himself.

So, to you who are such a great friend of God, this man fearfully approaches, doubtful of his salvation and even more certain of his great sinfulness, yet hoping in your even greater grace. Yes, greater than my sin, sir, is your grace. Besides, I know that what you can achieve before God can surely erase all my iniquity. So, good lord, since grace has made you such a good friend of God, this anxious soul flees to you.

My iniquity has reckoned me guilty before God, but grace has made you so blessed, while wickedness has made me so miserable. Truly, lord, I confess that my iniquity makes me what I now am, but you too did not make yourself into what you now are but, rather, the grace of God has fashioned you. So remember, kind sir, that just as God's grace has elevated you, your mercy toward me can raise me up out of my guilt.

Woe is me and what I have made myself to be. What I was meant to be, God, You made, but I have remade myself.[26] Into sin have I been conceived and

---

[26] Anselm is perhaps echoing Augustine once again here. In a sermon on loving one's neighbor, Bishop Augustine has his congregation imagine God's addressing them, asking them to think about one of their enemies, and then hearing the Lord say: "Behold: your enemy is a human person, so tell me—how is he your enemy? . . . It's not his being human that makes that person your enemy, for I made that! I made your neighbor human not bad, but he chose to become malicious through

born (Ps 51:5), but You washed me clean and You sanctified me. But I have sullied myself all the more. Perhaps it was necessary that I was born in sin, but now I wrap myself up in my sins fully and freely. Out of mercy I was led out of sin by You, but I have led myself miserably back into them. From them I was dutifully redeemed, but back into them I have disobediently returned.

You have cleansed this soul, loving God, a soul wounded by its first parents, but I, being so unrighteous, put to death what you had healed. Merciful Lord, remove the tattered rags of original sin and dress me in a robe of innocence, promising the new man incorruptibility (cf. 1 Cor 15:42–54). I have rejected what You had given me, and I brought sordid iniquity about in my very self, thus despising what you had promised. I hate what You promise me, and I instead choose the pains of eternal misery! Yet You had made the son of Your wrath into the son of Your grace (cf.

---

disobedience, following the devil—this is what makes this person your enemy, what he has done to himself" (*Sermon* 90.9). What God has made is good without qualification, what beings with free will have remade out of God's gift is where sin and the disfiguring of human nature occurs.

Rom 9:21–23), but I mocked that and instead made myself a son of Your hatred. You reformed Your loveable image in me, and I superimposed an image upon it that is loathsome. Woe, woe, whose—whose?—image did you superimpose upon God's image, you wretched and demented little man?[27]

Oh why is it not embarrassing to discuss that which I am so afraid of? Why did I hate to become like the one whose name scares me so?[28] He simply fell, but I chose to become debauched. He, with no previous sin needing vindication, fell through his pride; I, having seen his punishment but being so superficial, rushed headlong into my own sin. He

---

[27] Matthew 22:15–22 records the incident between Jesus and the Herodians regarding paying the Temple tax. Throughout the centuries, Christian commentators have understood this exchange to be a discussion about the image of God on every human soul, not ultimately answerable to Caesar and the ways of this world.

[28] Here Anselm is talking about the one from whom all humanity originates, the first Adam. The first human, as Anselm sympathetically casts it, was tempted directly by Satan (Gn 3) and fell due to the capital sin of pride not fully knowing what such divine aversion would entail. Anselm, on the other hand, knows clearly the effects of the Fall and chooses to turn away from God nonetheless, making him the far worse sinner.

had been established in innocence and I was restored to it; so, he had sinned against the One Who had created him, but I sinned against the One Who both created *and* re-created me. That one abandoned God and God allowed him to go, but I fled from God and He chased after me all the more; he persisted in his wickedness and God rejected him, while I rushed into sin and God kept calling me back. He hardened his heart and paid the price, I blocked God, but he tried to woo me back. Both of us are against God. He is against God, but God does not stand in need of him; I am against God, but God comes to die for me.

Oh unhappy, so exceedingly unhappy little man, if all of your humanity has not fled from you, it is so malice has a place to enter your inhumanity. Behold the one whose image I was horrified to see, but now see in myself many things even more horrible. Get away from me, get away, you who are now made up of what horrible substance I do not know. Flee even from yourself! You should be afraid of who you are. But, alas, you cannot escape yourself. You cannot even look at yourself because you are unable to bear it. For if you could tolerate such self-examination without the horror of pain, you would find even your tolerance intolerable. But insofar as you can admit this, you are more like the first sinner and thus intolerable to God.

This is not fortitude but flatness; it is not sanity but stiff-necked sin; it does not stem from consolation but from damnation. Not without an immense uproar of the heart are you able to tolerate the internal horror of your countenance, and because you are not able to flee it, you can neither stand to look at yourself nor tolerate yourself.

But see how it gets even worse if I do not look at myself, for I know that I am wrong. Oh, distress too great: if I examine myself, I am not able to bear myself, but if I do not examine myself, I can never know myself. Yet if I see myself as I am—intolerable horror, but if I don't see myself—inevitable condemnation. Here there is evil, but even worse, evil all around.

Miserable is the man tormented by a conscience he cannot escape; yet even more miserable is the man awaiting a condemnation which he cannot avoid. Unduly unhappy is the one who is horrible to himself, but much more unhappy is the one for whom death is eternally pressing. Amazingly agonized is the one who lives in continuous fear of his own ugliness. Such a one will be tormented by eternal anguish for his iniquity—evil here and evil there, too much here and too much there.

What an evil and sulfurous thing it is to sin. Sins, how easy you are to commit but how hard you are to stop.[29] Sinners, how easy you begin and how hard you become entrenched. Understand, understand, how evil and bitter it is to have let go of the Lord. Return, all you who sin, and do not allow your wills to sin again. Refuse, I say, refuse—it is evil and wretched to sin, so just refuse!

Sin is truly bitter and malicious, and in this I am quite experienced, about this I know. For either the unceasing pains torment my life as my penance or eternal tortures will trouble my life as my punishment. Either way, both are evil and both are bitter. And surely does the guilty one who stands before God is just stretched between each evil—and what

---

[29] Once again, we hear Anselm switch from talking to God or to one of His saints to speaking directly to the personification of one of his sins. But here he then goes on to address the entire race of sinners, offering almost a mini sermon on the importance of fleeing temptations.

is even worse—overwhelming evil, too much evil, too much evil. But this all arranged rightly, rightly arranged and justly, my Judge—and of course it is, for You are my God and my Lord and my Creator.

Take, then, Creator, take all this evil away from Your creature, if he is ever to thank You for causing him to exist. Rescue, Lord, Your servant from all these evils, if he is ever to confess You as his Lord. Save your sinner, God, so he would never doubt Your goodness. For even though I may have offended the Judge like that first sinner already had, at least I do not hate You as he did, nor do I despise your goodness.

As such, renew in me the grace of Your baptism through the great merit of Your baptizer. May Your grace go before me and may Your mercy follow after me. Give me back through my grieving what You had first given to me in the sacrament of Baptism. Give to the one who pleads what You have given to the ignorant. Reform the face which I have disgraced; restore the innocence which I have violated. You Who take away the sins of the world, take away the sins I brought into the world when I was born, and then take away the sins I have committed while living this life.

Take away the sins of the world, because these sins of the world are those which I carry from my conduct in the world. Take away, You Who take away the sins of the world (Jn 1:29–32), through the merits of Him who shows You to the world by this testimony: Take away the sins which I have contracted in the world. Take from me whatever is not from You, because I hate that which is just of me, hoping in You.[30]

And you, St. John—you are the John who showed the world the One Who takes away the sins of the world—through that grace bestowed upon you, obtain for me that mercy which takes away my sins. You, God, take away the sins of the world and you, his friend, say: "Here is He who takes away the sins of the world (Jn 1:29–32); behold the One before you who is weighed down with the world's sins." You take away sins, and thus

---

[30] Anselm again contrasts what is from God (goodness, truth, beauty) and what has come from his own self (that which is despicable and in need of healing).

proclaim: "Behold Me Who takes away your sins, just as John proclaims."

Behold the Doctor and the one who testifies to Him; behold the sick servant of the Doctor along with his work, and let's beg the Doctor and His witness. True Doctor, I pray that You make me whole. And you, His true witness, I ask that you pray for me. Prove it to me in me: Jesus, You by Your healing and you, John, by your proclamation. Let me experience what I hear and let me have what I believe. Jesus, good Lord, if You can do what he testifies you can, let Your healing be in me. John, you who point God out to us, and since you testify to what He can do, let your word take root in me. Heal me, Lord, for healing belongs to You. Obtain this for me, Lord, for You alone can secure my healing, for You are the great Lord and you, John, "are great in the sight of the Lord" (Lk 1:15).

Jesus, You can achieve all things simply by Who You are; and you, John, are truly powerful because you remain near Him. You are the supreme and good God, and you are His worthy good friend who is the eternally merciful and blessed God. Amen.

Questions for Prayerful Reflection

- Have you incorporated John the Baptist into your prayer life? What does he mean for you? Read the workings of God as John is brought into this world: Jn 1:5–25, 57–80. Meditate slowly on John 1:67–79, "The Canticle of Zechariah." What most resonates with you in this song of praise? Why?
- John represents the power of littleness in the Christian story: we meet him in the womb, he spends his life in the desert, and then dies alone while in prison. Do you appreciate how Jesus chooses to work through the power of what the world considers insignificant—the unborn, the meeting of mothers, and so on? How could this impact how you see what is truly godly, and how might this affect how you pray and live out your Christian vocation?
- What might it mean for you to feel Jesus's healing "in" yourself, as Anselm begs?

What is in you that is in need of Jesus's healing touch?

Prayer to Mary Magdalene

In a series of homilies on the Gospels, Pope Gregory the Great (d. 604) was among the first to cast Mary Magdalene as the first to proclaim the Good News of Jesus's resurrection and the life-changing consequences of that original Easter morn: "Go to my brothers and tell them, 'I am going to my Father and your Father, to my God and your God'" (Jn 20:17). During Anselm's time, Pope Gregory's good instincts developed even further, even to the point of St. Thomas Aquinas calling her "an apostle to the Apostles" (apostolorum apostola), using that term literally as one "sent out" and not as anything to do with the apostolic succession of priests and bishops (Thomas Aquinas, Commentary on the Gospel of John, chap 20, lecture III, 6).

Such medieval devotion is first found in Anselm's prayer here (numbered sixteen in his collection), seeing in Mary's love an affection for Jesus which would cleanse her from all sin and undo the toxic work of Eve. In the following prayer, it becomes clear that Jesus loved Mary not despite her sins but precisely because of them, giving her a tender heart and a vulnerability deeply aware of how she needed a Savior—providing hope for the contrite Anselm and, in turn, for all of us still today.

Anselm's affection for Mary Magdalene emboldens him, even to the point of challenging Christ's words to her, asking why she was crying and wondering for whom she is in search. But the resolution comes in a psychological insight when Anselm realizes Jesus was neither ignorant nor chastising Mary but knowing her heart deeply (for He had created it). Jesus knew the only way she could tell her story was through sighing, sobbing, and stammering.

Oh, holy Mary Magdalene, you have come to Christ the font of mercy with your own font of tears. From Him your burning thirst was fully slaked; you, a sinner, have been justified by Him, and by Him, your bitter pain has been sweetly relieved. You certainly see in your own soul, my most dear lady, how a sinful woman can be made one with her Creator, what guidance such a miserable soul needs, and what medicine restores such a languishing soul to wholeness.

My dear friend of God, it is enough to know that you are the one to whom "many sins have been forgiven because she has shown great love" (Lk 7:47).

Oh, most blessed Lady, I—a most sinful man—do not think of your sins as a rebuke, but I imagine them as an act of immense mercy, as having been absolved. Of this I am confident, or else I would despair; this is my hope, or else I might perish. I myself say this, miserably thrown down into the depths of all my vices, weighed down by the weight of my iniquities. I myself have been exiled into the shadowy prison of my own sins, encircled by the deadness of darkness.

You are chosen because you are loved and loved because you are God's chosen. So, to you, most blessed, I—a miserable man—call out: I, who am in gloom, beg for light, a sinner pleading for salvation, one unclean calling to be made pure. Remember, most kindly lady, what you once were and how you longed for mercy, and acquire for me that same extravagant kindness which you received when desired. Obtain for me that same devout contrition, those tears of humility, a desire for heaven as my true homeland and a disdain of being exiled here on earth, the sting of repentance, and a fear of eternal damnation. Produce for me, dearest lady, that same intimacy which you not only had but still enjoy before the Font of Mercy.

Draw me to Him so I can wash away my sins. Bring me to Him so my thirst may be quenched. Pour over me those waters which alone can refresh my dryness. For you, it will not be difficult to obtain whatever you desire from your tremendously loving and gracious Lord, Your friend Who lives and reigns!

But You, most godly Lord, why do You ask her why she cries (see Jn 20:13)? Surely it is apparent to You how her heart as well as her soul's sweet life has been heartlessly butchered. Oh, a holiness to be admired, woe a lawlessness to be shuddered at: for You were stretched out on a Cross like a thief fixed there with iron nails like a joke for the unrighteous. And You say, "Woman, why are you weeping?" (Jn 20:13). She could not keep them from murdering You, but she thought she could at least honor Your corpse with oils to keep it from decaying.

She was not able to talk to You when You were still alive, so she was at least able to weep over You when You were dead. Herself feeling so close to death, she could at least now recite in mournful murmurings that life-giving teaching she had heard when You were alive. But now even that corpse, which she would have been happy to hold, she thinks has been taken from her, and yet You say, "Woman, why are you weeping?" Oh, the ravages of deep sorrow! For she had seen with her own eyes—if she had been able to watch—what cruel men so cruelly did to You, and now she believes that she has lost even what remained of You from their cruel hands.

Every hope she had held on to fled because now she is not even able to hold Your remains which were to remind her of You, and someone asks: "Whom are you looking for?" (Jn 20:15a), "Why are you weeping?" (Jn 20:15b). But shouldn't You, her singular joy, be the last to increase her sorrow? But You know and You desire it to be so, understanding that she is not able to tell her story, a story of such lament, unless it was to be told in stammering words and broken sighs. For You are not unaware of the love You drew from her. You know her through and through, for You are that gardener (see Jn 20:15c) Who planted her soul in your garden. And I see how You tend to what You plant. So do You water her, or are You testing her? Ah, but truly, I can say that You are both tending and testing her.[31]

[31] Anselm's insight here really is psychologically profound: Jesus knows exactly how to spur each of our hearts, and He

But certainly a dutiful love could neither bear her weeping nor bear to hide itself any longer. The kindness of charity thus steps forth, lest the bitterness of tears drowns her. The Lord uses the name of His handmaid which she knows and she recognizes the voice of her Lord. I think or rather certainly affirm that she sensed Your tender-heartedness by which she is used to being called, "Mary" (Jn 20:16a). O sweet voice, so pleasant, how much she sensed such love. He could not have called out to her any more succinctly or any more quickly. "I know who you are and what it is you desire, behold Me; do not weep, but behold Me Whom you seek."

Immediately her tears changed, not dried up at once, I believe, but certainly slowed down—for when they once sprung from a heart tortured by sadness, now they flow from a heart exulting with joy. Oh,

---

comes to us precisely in the way He knows will most spur us on to receiving and loving Him. One can easily wonder why He waited a week to appear to Thomas (who obviously needed to sit for a time with his doubts) and first come to the Apostles when Thomas alone is away (see Jn 20:19–29). Here, Anselm likewise sees how Jesus challenges Mary but does so in order to help her lower her guard and speak of her love in the way she does best, with tears and testing (Jn 20:11–18).

what a contrast between "Rabbouni" (Jn 20:16b) and "If you carried Him away, tell me" (Jn 20:15c). Oh, what dissonance between "They have taken my Lord, and I don't know where they laid Him" (Jn 20:13) and "I have seen the Lord and He told me all these things" (Jn 20:18).

But since I am wretched and without love, how shall I presume to describe the love of God as well as the love of a holy friend of God? For indeed, how will a good heart be pleasantly perfumed unless it has tasted within itself that same sweetness? Truly, You Who are Truth itself know me through and through, my Lord, my Most Sweet Jesus, and You can verify how I compose this prayer out of love for Your love.

I desire that You ignite Your love in me so that I may desire to love You alone as You have commanded (see Mt 22:37), and then I can offer to You my troubled soul, "a contrite, humbled heart" (Ps 51:19). Give to me, Lord, while I remain in exile the bread of tears and sorrow, longing for them more than any abundance of earthly delicacies.

On account of Your love and on account of the tender merits of Your sweet Mary along with Your most Blessed Mother, the even greater Mary, hear me. Do not, most holy Redeemer Jesus, despise the prayer of a sinner so unworthy, but come with Your grace to strengthen one who loves You so. Wrench my heart from its torpor and through Your burning love, give me the grace to reach the contemplation of Your eternal glory where You live and reign with the Father and the Holy Spirit, God for ever and ever.

Questions for Prayerful Reflection

- Read the accounts of Mary Magdalene in the New Testament (Jn 20:11–18): What do her encounters with Jesus tell you about your faith? What about Mary most resonates with you and your friendship with Christ?
- How does Jesus best come to you? What people, what experiences, what prayers and songs, or any simple moments most fill you with God's holy Presence? What has made this point of contact so special for you? Trace your history and pray about why God best meets you there.
- Are you ever brought to tears while encountering the Lord? If so, reflect on

the last time you wept before God and, first, thank Him for such holy hunger and, second, ask yourself what most often moves you to cry.

Prayer to St. John the Evangelist, Composed by a Man Afraid of Being Damned

Along with Mary the Mother of God and Mary Magdalen, John the Evangelist was the only recorded Apostle to have stood under the Cross while Jesus breathed His last. Anselm composed two prayers (numbers eleven and twelve) for John the Evangelist—the first composed out of a fear of being forgotten by God and the second composed out of a fear that true affection induces in the heart of the lover. The first is what Augustine called servile fear, the trepidation that one simply doesn't matter in another's eyes; the second Augustine considered "chaste fear," teaching how every lover fears the loss of being in the presence of his or her beloved. Anselm continues this prayer and pleads to John for the needed graces he can obtain through his intercession, graces that would keep Anselm always in God's presence and favor.

Saintly and blessed John, most exalted of God's Gospel writers, most beloved of the Apostles, so advanced in the love of God among all His beloved people—and, being so superabundantly loved has become your unique mark among us all. For you are that John, the one who so familiarly rested upon the heart of the Most High (cf. Jn 13:23), and when He was dying and would have to be away from His mother in the body, He relied on you to be a substitute son for her. To you, oh blessed one, so amicable and so loved by God, I have been judged by Him as a nothing-of-a-man, so I beg you for prayers. Then, through the intercession of one so cherished, pray that I might avoid God's approaching wrath.

For this sinner's crimes compel him to seek an intercessor, sir, and so he hastens toward your renowned intimacy with God Whom he fears could be his Punisher. Because of the power you possess due to that same intimacy, it is certain, my lord, that you are able to do what you desire before God. Hoping in your loving care, I know you will not despise a sinner who so desperately cries out to you, and thus I turn to you, as lukewarm as I am. With all my heart's affection, I presume to call upon your powerful intercession for my sinful soul so that it might be saved from those torments which attract all the countless evils in it.

But alas, wretched me, how all these faults of mine promise me what I really don't desire (cf. Rom 7:15–20). But, behold, I try to be encouraged by your friendship with God (cf. Jn 15:15), and then I become even more downcast and deterred because of my depravity with Him. And you, God's own beloved, whenever I sin against your Beloved, certainly I deserve your disgust as well. Oh, unconscionable sin, for when I sin against God, I am offending not only God Himself but also offending all who intercede before Him! It must be true that not only is the one who commits crimes against God hated not only by God's friends but also by God Himself and even by all of His creatures.

My sins, my sins, oh the more I think about you, the more you terrify me! So where are you abducting him, where are you taking this wretched little man that you have so long seduced?[32] How deep has he fallen and how low will this unhappy soul be cast down in following you? What will he lose and what

[32] In a typical Anselmian move, he here again takes up discourse with his sins.

agonies will he gain, forced from the love of God which he once held through his innocence but is now driven by your malice into becoming a horror to God and to all of His creatures?

However, if sins result in an all-encompassing filth that pulls the sinner away from God, from that place in God where He hides Himself, how could God ever reveal Himself to someone like that, to someone who is hardly a man weighed down by the burden of his sins which he just cannot let go of, someone so hideous and reeking with the injuries and wounds of his crime which he cannot heal?[33]

This is the sort of person who comes to you, John—beloved friend of God—this is the state of my soul which comes before you: yes, this, this is my misery—oppressed by my sins because I have made of myself such a friend to the world, and thus now stand as an enemy to God. Alas this name, "enemy of

---

33 Where does God "hide Himself"? The Latin phrase here *Deus se abscondat*—God hides Himself—is both biblical as well as a standard way early medievals explained how God oftentimes chooses to deal with the stubbornly sinful: "Rather, it is your crimes that separate you from your God, it is your sins that make him hide his face so that he does not hear you" (Is 59:2; cf., Ez 39:23; Mic 3:4).

God," a name hated by all. Oh, how unfortunately it comes from me, but how rightly it is attributed to me! The tribulations: the truth of things convicts me as an enemy of God, and an immense horror stops me from admitting it.[34]

Such distress: I have provoked God, and now all things long to take revenge on me, and no one or nothing remains to intercede on my behalf. Sorrows, pains, groans, and shrieks: where are you present if you are absent here? Where are you on fire if here you are lukewarm? May my body be torn asunder by torments, let my affections be consumed with burning, and let there be a tumult in my innermost being if only God would look upon my wretchedness with mercy.

---

[34] Notice the intentional choice of biblical language here. The Holy Spirit, Anselm knows, "convicts" the Christian of sin, He does not "condemn" the sinner. Condemn means to "damn," while convict means to "conquer," and that is why Jesus tells us that when the Spirit "comes he will convict the world in regard to sin" (Jn 16:8). Too, St. Paul teaches the legal-bound Romans, "Hence, now there is no condemnation for those who are in Christ Jesus" (Rom 8:1). The Spirit's presence in Anselm's prayers is to console us and while the Holy Spirit may help point out our sins, He does so in order to give us the grace to conquer them, never to belittle or shame us.

Oh, you merciful friends of God, take compassion upon one so lacking in that same mercy which God has granted to you. Hurry to help me so God's anger does not overtake me along with His enemies. I resist it and I detest it; in fact, I abhor being called an enemy of God, but still admit that I have sinned. If only someone would rush to my aid.

You are that disciple whom Jesus loved, and you should admit this is your special trait, and this is why I beg you for the same love, recognizing my need for your help, St. John. John, if you are that disciple whom Jesus loved, I ask that because of such intimacy, I might be the sinner whom Jesus absolves through you. If that glorious breast was a familiar place for you to rest your head (cf. Jn 13:23), I ask that because of such tenderness, it may become a place of salvation for me too.

I confess, my lord and beloved of God, that you are right to be angry with me who has sinned against God your Beloved, but for sure the Lord will spare one who cries out to Him on account of His friend. Therefore, oh blessed John, gifted with such love from God, His guilty servant begs that you can reconcile me to Him. Oh, God's beloved, your helping the guilty in no way challenges God's love, for you are not harboring him but only interceding for him. For I am only asking for your intercession, and by making my confession, I am not asking for you to obtain a defense of my iniquity.

Friend of God, do not consider this sinner God's enemy or yours, for he believes and confesses God to be your friend with as much love as he can offer. If I believe, if I confess, and if I want to love such a great love of God as that which has been granted to you, and so I beg of you through this grace which has been granted to you: turn the hatred of God away from me, even though I do deserve it. Do this, good sir, on account of how much you are loved; do this because I too am His work, His servant, and His redeemed one. Do this on account of Who God is and do this with Him. Do this so that what He has brought into being is not lost, so that what He has redeemed does not perish. Do this since you truly love all His works and confess His blessed Name.

Jesus, against Whom I have certainly sinned, Lord, Whom I have so vilely held in contempt, Omnipotent One, Whose wrath I have provoked due to my pride—You are the Lover of John Your beloved Apostle, and to him, I—your panic-stricken and accused sinner—flee. Your sinner, Your offender, regardless how criminal and regardless how iniquitous, also holds on tightly to the name "Your beloved" between himself and the impending sentence of Your just judgment. On account of Your blessed love, spare the one who seeks Your protection. Lord, under what mantle can he find protection if under the name of "Your beloved" there is still persecution? Where is there refuge if under Your love there is still danger?

Lord, do not let one who flees to Your love feel your hatred. Lord, Lord, do not let my wickedness which earns damnation outrun Your grace which merits mercy. Good, Good God, may Your repugnance with me not bring what You have created to naught, but let Your love spare the servant whom You have redeemed. Kindliest God, Who "hates nothing which you have made" (Wis 11:24), behold him whom You have made and whom You have saved.

Why will You damn him if You do not hate him, Lord, for he accuses himself and calls out to You? Accomplish this, Good Lord, because of him whom

You most familiarly loved among all Your disciples. Do not be my Condemner because You alone are my Savior. Blessed are You, forever and ever.

Questions for Prayerful Reflection

- Of the four creatures (called a tetramorph—a being with four faces) depicted in Ezekiel's vision (Ez 1:10) as well as John's epiphany of the same four creatures (Rev 4:7), John is always represented as the eagle because his theology "soars" above the other Gospel authors. Read John's Prologue (John 1) and let any image or word that resonates with you simply sit in your soul and ask God why this is so attractive to you at this point in your life.
- What does it mean to be called Jesus's friend? Philosophers since Plato have defined a friend as "another self," and that is what God has become in the humanity of Jesus Christ, another "you." Have you ever considered how Christ has become like you so you can become like Him?

How might your Christ-centered life imagine Him more as a friend who enjoys your company than an Overlord who is rarely happy with you?

- What parts of your soul, your past, most resonate with Anselm's sense of impending doom and fear of being judged? Where you are afraid, is that rational when you step back and look at your life? Have you confessed this memory? Can you finally let go of it?

Prayer to St. John the Evangelist, Pleading for God's Love and Those Near Him

The second Johannine prayer focuses on John as one who is known as "the beloved." Can you, however, imagine God's love for you being the same as John's? The difference might be that John allows himself to be loved, while most of us turn away from the intimacy and the vulnerability being another's beloved entails. The main goal of this prayer, fittingly, is to increase our receptivity and reciprocated love of God. To achieve this, Anselm portrays himself as a destitute beggar who stands incessantly before a great and wealthy donor.

St. John, you are that John who is one of the great apostles of God, one of the great princes of the Reign of God, the one who is the most richly loved by God (cf. Jn 11:3, 5) and who loves Him with the same love: behold how opulent such divine blessings are and how rich you are with such blessed opulence. But now behold this soul which is agonizing but is Christian, poor and in need of those riches with which you have been richly blessed. Starving, this soul pounds at the door of your mercy; poor and in need, this soul begs the almsgiving of your abundance. From the undiminishable storehouse of which is sufficient for you and for so many, impart to this soul as much as it needs to live.

Extend from the rich storeroom of your soul, rich friend of God, extend to the soul of a poor servant of God—Who so loves you—that which might not be much to you but is so great to me (cf. Mt 13:51–53), what is easy for you but essential for me. I am certainly poor, my lord, beloved of Our Lord, my soul is poor, and I am compelled and blush having to confess this. Such a soul fails in the love of God twice: (1) it loves God much less than it should and (2) it lets itself be loved by God so much less than it needs. Without a doubt, I confess that, on the one hand, I am truly unjust but, on the other hand, God is not, and in both instances, I see how I am most miserable before God's just judgment.

In saying this, You just and merciful God, I am neither forgetting nor am I ungrateful for all Your many, many blessings to me from the very start of my being created, but my hungering soul will always call itself poor and needy until it is satisfied by Your love. For sure, this is one of the greatest and most pleasing gifts You offer to me: due to having sweetly tasted Your love, my soul is so awakened that it "refuses to be comforted" (Ps 77:3) unless it is filled by You. So, to obtain it, since the cry of Your least beloved sinner is so insufficient, I call upon great merits by imploring John, Your much beloved-lover.

Therefore, You Who are good Sweetness and sweet Goodness, because of Whom all things are good, turn John to me and You to him; rather, may You and he both turn to me that through you both I might obtain this desired good of your satiety. I know, Lord, I know, and I confess that I am not worthy to be loved by You, but certainly You are not unworthy to be loved by me. Give me, therefore, my Lord, by his merits, from whom Thou are worthy, and I shall be made worthy from where I am now unworthy.[35] But he prays for me more mightily because—being Your beloved, Lord Jesus—he can do this more effectively. Reclining against Your loving heart (cf. Jn 13:23), he prays for me, and in that place You hear my desire because of him who is so united with You.

Saint John, beloved of Jesus Christ my Lord, the servant of your friend implores you, that on account of the name of his Lord, your Beloved, you might acquire for him that twofold love of God: that is, I pray that you can retrieve for me the worthiness to be loved by Him and that I might be made worthy to love Him in return.

For certainly, God's beloved, if He loves us for your sake, you will extend His mercy to us, and if

---

[35] "Lord, I am not worthy that you should enter under my roof, but only say the word and my soul shall be healed." (Mt 8:8). This line from a Roman centurion is used before every Holy Communion, teaching two essential truths: no child of Adam is worthy to approach the Almighty—no one has done enough, merited enough, been good enough—but, secondly and infinitely more importantly, when the Word of God freely approaches, we must allow Him to enter and thus transform us. It is He Who makes us worthy, and our task, as Anselm knows, is to allow Him in all humility and openness.

we love Him on account of you, you will graciously repay Him. Certainly, good sir, if you turn Him to loving us, you make us all the more indebted to you, and if you can stir us to love God more, you make yourself the one who has paid our debt too.

Blessed John, no matter how much you do to make Him love so many, there is no less love for you, and whatever you do to make so many love Him, you pay back their debt all the more. So have mercy, sir, on this beggar of yours, since I am so indebted to you for such a good and that you might return a soul to God. Accomplish this, I pray, lord, do it! For if you fail to accomplish this renewal, nothing but condemnation will be the result. So, save your servant by the grace given to you so by His glory, he may come to God.

Most beloved disciple of piety, why would you who are so rich reject one so poor, you so powerful refuse one so needy, which would be noxious to no one and be of so much good to the injured party? For if my sins block what I desire, would not your merits assist me in my prayer so much more? Do my sins have the power to harm while your merits prove powerless to help? Excuse me, good sir, if I feel forced to feel what I am afraid to say.

If so, why would what I ask for be negated on account of my sins when my request is based not on my merits but yours? Why, I ask, might this be so if the merits offered to Him (by you) are greater than the sins which offend Him (by me)? For I am certain, lord, that—if you wish—your grace is worth so much more with God your Lover than all my sins which He has absolved, and in loving me, He will make me His beloved too.

Therefore, blessed John, see that He Who loves you loves me too. Do this through that breadth of charity which you have taught and possess and which you would never hold back from anyone, desiring the common good in which you now rejoice. Do this for the love you owe Him, and in so doing, you can also repay my love along with yours to Him, to Whom not only you are indebted, but oh so many.

Blessed John, you have certainly experienced your own belovedness. And just as no one can give back to God before he is indebted to God, no one is able to return more than what he has been given (Jn 3:27). If, therefore, many men and women love your Loving God through you, they in no way could ever pay back that debt: I thus pray, sir, please do not cast anyone off who begs you to be numbered among those debtors. Instead, ignite his tepid love and return it to him on fire! Help me thus to shine brightly and hear my prayer.

Jesus, Lord, Whom I desire to hear, and John, whose intercession I request, my desire so compels me that my heart longs to compel you both. Surely my doing this is not inevitable but is taken up spontaneously, not unwillingly but willingly. Be patient, therefore, and spare me—and if love devises anything, let it implement love.[36]

Support me, I say, because my loving the Love of God compels me (see 2 Cor 5:14). Lord and good sir, I believe and I know that you two love one another, but how might I also experience this if you refuse to

---

36 In having a creature who is also fully God, a God Who is also fully creature, love can never compete against love in Christianity. Loving God is the only way to love neighbor, and loving neighbor is really the only way to love God (see 1 Jn 4:20). If that is so, then, one never needs to worry about loving too much or too many, but must, of course, be alert to how love can morph into various imitations. Here Anselm prays that if love desires anything, it is for an increase in more love—a request never made in competition or in a spirit of entitlement.

grant what I now ask of you both? Jesus, how could I ever prove Your love for John or for me if through him You fail to concede to what I seek—which is, to be loved by you both and to love you both in return. John, how can I know Jesus loves you if you do not obtain for me to be loved as well? Or that you love Jesus if you do not help me to love Him as well?

Excuse my excessiveness, Love of God, for it is Your love which compels me to speak in such a manner. Therefore, You, oh God, and you, His beloved John, do not love only yourselves in your blessedness but love us in our misery. May we share your joy, as you have shared our sufferings. Do not hoard such a good only for yourselves but let all this goodness and joy flow over us too; let it diffuse from within us and thus make our souls happy.

Lover and beloved of God, St. John—made safe in that blessed fullness of glory of your love for one another, be attentive to this pauper who also begs for this twofold love of God. Bestow this upon him as much as you can, for you possess this in a greater abundance, and you see me wallowing in my poverty. You know well what you, lord, have written down in your Epistle, admonishing that no one who, having the riches of the world and seeing that his brother or sister is in need should "close his bowels of compassion" from him (1 Jn 3:17).[37]

What then, sir, if one partaking in the nature of eternal life (cf. 2 Pt 1:4) sees that the soul of his neighbor is still in need, would he close his innermost being to him? Merciful master, if you had wanted "the bowels of compassion" of the men who own this world's goods not be closed to those in need, surely this is even more true for those who enjoy even greater goods toward those whose needs are much greater than earthly wants? Behold, I hear you command men's insides to relax, and I see that you have the heart of loving God and of being loved by God, and you clearly see the need of my own soul.

So look: you are the one having or even commanding the needy right before you, gazing at one another. If therefore, kind sir, your vision has more holiness than my devout prayer, let your vision

---

[37] Anslem's Vulgate Bible has *viscera* here, from which we obviously get the word "visceral." It literally means one's "insides," "guts," or "bowels," an idiom which might sound odd to our ears today but 1 John 3:17 is trying to teach us that compassion must come from deep within, from the core of our being or, as we are more comfortable saying, from the heart.

become my prayer. For you did not write, "If anyone sees his brother or sister praying and closes his bowels" but, "If anyone sees his brother or sister in need." Do this, then, lord, for you see my need and indeed you see just that.

Oh soul, my soul, gather all your affection together and bring it before him. Shout and cry out from the depths of your being before John: "See me!" And then repeat again and again, "Notice me, notice me!" And, John, you certainly do see, and you see me! Therefore, look again at me, sir—see me and know me, see me and have pity.

See and know. See so that I may know that you realize my deep need. See so that I may know your tender care. See, see me, since you no doubt do see me.[38] I know immediately, and I even feel that you see me. I know, I feel. Oh, how my understanding rushes into what it hears: because you have

[38] Even Mother Mary declares, Behold me! Transparency and a willingness to be "seen" is a grace of the saint who trusts God with the core of her or his being, unafraid to be known and touched at the most hidden or even embarrassing parts of one's soul. Mary freely and purely provides this example of being approached for sinners who find it much more difficult because of their misdeeds.

commanded my brother to "open his heart," I wonder whether I am that brother or even a neighbor, but I dare not assert what I wish to be, unwilling to claim what is not properly mine.

Jesus, John's teacher, look upon us. Lord, my thirsty soul aches alongside this stream, but there is nothing for it to drink unless it flows from Your fountain. So, let Your fountain of mercy flow from You into John, that I may drink of You through him (cf. Jn 4:13–14; Eph 5:18). Good Jesus, respond for me: I am returning to the Source, and can go no further. For while a soul is next to this Living Font, no one can dry up and perish. So, let no one stand between those like me who thirst and this Source—for those who are filled can hear Your command, and those who are thirsty long to drink of Your clemency from this Source.

Say to him, "John, who appears to you to be the neighbor who had fallen among thieves" (Lk 10:30)?[39] Respond, blessed John, in the words of the

[39] Anselm here chooses to conclude his second prayer to John with the account of the Good Samaritan from the Gospel of Luke (Lk 10:25–37). This may seem like a clunky move but his intent here is to show that we are all called to be that Good

Samaritan who stands in for the entire human race, giving thanks to him: "Who was merciful to him" (Lk 10:37). Come, Good Jesus, for You have begun to aid my prayer, so now into Your hands I hand it over (cf. Lk 23:46), and since You are perfectly good, bring this prayer to completion. Tell Your beloved John, I ask, to see me, Your servant, and say to him, "Go, and you do the same" (Lk 10:37).

Oh my soul, hope and rejoice, rejoice and love: for St. John, whom you so hesitantly asked to hear you, is preparing an intercessor for you. As a mere pauper, you begged through another because you did not really trust him. However, look: he ran to you and prayed for you precisely where you were falling short. Oh goodness, Oh mercy, Oh love! See how much John shows you that he loves you, and how much he stirs you, my soul, to love him in return! Therefore, wait and hope—not for yourself but for John, because he will hear your desire and finish your prayer this way: "My heart and my flesh,"

Samaritan by linking John's call to give from the core of our being to the conclusion of the prayer which supposedly marks our going back into the world where every soul is our neighbor worthy of our care.

rejoice in him and love him, "and all that is within me" (Ps 84:3), bless him, amen.

Questions for Prayerful Reflection

- Can you relate to Anselm's confession that nothing in this world will satisfy his heart? As you have aged, have you reprioritized what you once felt to be essential? All things pass, which does not make them unimportant, but such transience demands we have our hearts set first and foremost on the One whose allure and importance never ends. Review your past and list the ways you have been cleansed of being worldly or—even creaturely—centered.
- Do you ever compete for love? Is love for you a "zero sum" reality? Notice how Anselm admits that if St. John intercedes for him to acquire more of God's love, "no matter how much you do to make Him love so many, there is not less love for you."

- Is waiting hard? Not being in charge, not having your needs or even desires met when and how you might prefer is ultimately an admittance of our own littleness and worldly insignificance. Think about a time you were impatient and search your soul for why. Then pray over being open to the grace next time that happens, to offer your impatience back to the Father as an imitation and extension of His Son's own.

Prayer to St. Peter

Number nine in Anselm's collection is the lone prayer to Peter, Prince of the Apostles. Throughout it, Anselm draws widely from all the images used for Peter in the Christian Tradition—shepherd, absolver of sins, the gate for the elect, and so on. We are again introduced to the splendor of a saint by means of the wretchedness of a sinner. As the prayer moves on, however, hope emerges. Drawing from the first pope's first letter (specifically 1 Peter 5:8), the devil may prowl like a lion, but the power of Christ instantiated in Peter is more than enough to ward off the inevitability of sin and death. It is, in fact, what keeps the entire Church from crumbling.

Perhaps that is why, more than any other saint, Anselm taps into the office of Peter for his strength. That is, it is not so much Peter's person that gives a sinner hope, for Peter himself has showed his infidelity and even denied the Lord three times publicly. What gives the sinner and, by extension, the entire Church hope is the office Peter wears and the power ensured by the Lord Himself: "And so I say to you, you are Peter, and upon this rock I will build my Church, and the gates of the netherworld shall not prevail against it" (Mt 16:18). This office is graciously imposed by Jesus upon Peter, despite his frailties, and—as Catholics attest—the same office imposed upon every pope whose office is to guide and govern God's people. It is not so much the man but the munus (the Latin for office or one's function). Of note for us today is the fact that the only feast in the liturgical year which officially names and celebrates an office and not just a personal feat of holiness is the office or Chair of Peter on February 22.

Holy and most kindly Peter, faithful pastor of God's sheep, prince of the Apostles and prince of these princes, who can bind and loosen as you so desire, who can heal and resuscitate whomever you will, who grants the heavenly kingdom to whomever you wish. Great Peter, great one, wealthy in such great and countless gifts, splendid in such great and countless dignities, behold: I am a little man, the poorest and lowliest of all, engulfed by countless and impossible sufferings, miserably in need of the help of your power. Yet my mouth lacks the words which only fail my need as it is, nor does my heart have such devotion that it could ever reach from my depths to your heights.

Yet again and again, I try to shake the lethargy from my mind, and I try to restrain my mind from wandering aimlessly with empty thoughts. But with all the strength it can muster, it is neither ever able to break free from the gloom of its own torpor—so entrenched as it is from the filth of its sins—nor can it stand for any period of time in the same prayerful intention. Alas, I am the most wretched of all wretches! This is indeed so, not feigned piety, but the reality. Who then can come to the aid of one so miserable, to one who so lacks the ability to express himself in words or show the sorrow of his mind?

Oh great Peter, if the clamor of my suffering does not reach up to you, allow your piety's attentiveness to descend down to me. Let my hardness be broken, my darkness be illumined, my wretchedness be seen. Look out, kind shepherd, for the sheep of the flock entrusted to you, and show pity to the misery in which this sheep labors. Do not treat him as his evils demand but treat him as his prayer pleads.

See the sick sheep who is stretched out groaning before the faithful shepherd, before the Lord of the shepherd and all his sheep. He returns as a stray, begging forgiveness for his waywardness and for his disobedience. He comes and shows the pious and healing shepherd the wolves' bitemarks and the lacerations of all the wounds incurred since running off. He also reveals the sores he suffered through long neglect, begging for pity while he still can draw a breath, and expressing his sorrow to the merciful pastor more by showing with actions than by imploring with words.

Good shepherd, Peter, do not make it difficult to approach you, and please don't turn your merciful eyes away from me. Look, I pray you, do not cast this penitent aside, do not wait to hear the prayers of this beggar. Because he has loathed the life-giving pasture, he languishes for want of strength, and since he has indulged in pestilence, he attracts deadly diseases. Full blown ulcers, pus-filled wounds, and putrid rot all drag him swiftly to his death. Wolves have fed on his blood and now they hide expectantly ready to pounce. His enemy "like a roaring lion" (1 Pt 5:8) circles ready to devour him.

Faithful shepherd, cast your eyes upon him and see how he has been entrusted to you. And even if he has wandered far, at least he never denied his Lord and Shepherd. Look well upon his countenance and see the sign of your Lord and his Lord.[40] Even if under so much squalor you do not recognize a face washed and cleansed in the baptismal font of Christ, at least acknowledge that he confesses the name of Christ, Who three times asked you if you loved Him and after three times of your confessing, Christ said, "Feed my sheep" (Jn 21:15–17). For certainly Jesus is the Lover of His sheep, Who discerns the love of His shepherd before He entrusts His sheep to him. And so, when you confessed that you were one who

---

[40] For the importance of being sealed with the Sign of the Cross as a rite of claiming one for Christ, even apart from Baptism, see Augustine, *Confessions* 1.11.17.

loved Him, He entrusted His sheep to you. If so, why could Christ's shepherd spurn one of His sheep?

Peter, pastor of Christ, gather up this sheep of Christ. Your Lord searched him out, found him, and now places him upon your shoulders rejoicing. Do not forsake him who has returned to you and is begging you. The Lord purchased him with His own blood even before this sheep was born, so his shepherd should not spurn him now that he has been reborn and is placed under your protection. Sadly, how long will it last that this sheep does not know that he has been received, washed clean, and held dear.

Holy Peter, if the name of "shepherd" and "sheep" does not move you, may the name of "apostle," "prince of the apostles," and the name "Christian soul" stir you to act! Of course, the sheep which I am offering you is my soul, a soul which has been reborn in the baptism of Christ. And these wounds, these sores, and those tears, which I told you about, these aren't found in just a sheep's flesh but in a rational soul. This hunger, this lack of toughness, these sufferings are not just in the belly of a sheep but in the mind of one made human. These wolves and lions are not four-footed creatures but actual demons.

And all these evils are the result of a lack of virtue and my sins piled high.

Since I do not feel I have yet been sufficiently heard, I shall anxiously repeat my story from its beginning. I shall even multiply my prayers. I shall set a faithful soul before the gatekeeper of the kingdom of heaven, the prince of the Apostles—a soul miserable because it resides in the kingdom of sin but gasps for the kingdom of heaven, and so it invokes Peter, the gatekeeper of that heavenly kingdom and the prince of the Apostles.

So, behold, merciful Peter, I present myself and reveal to you my soul with its nerves of virtue weakened and bound by the chains of vice. My soul is weighed down by the weight of its sins, fouled with the filth of its crimes, ripped asunder by the slashings of demons, rotten and fetid by the ulcers of its misdeeds, overwhelmed and oppressed by all of these and even other hellish evils which you can see better than I how they have left me needy, oppressed, enveloped and overwhelmed, and destitute of all good.

See how I am a miserable soul and Peter is an Apostle full of mercy—both before the merciful God Who showed mercy to the Apostle Peter, teaching him what he needed to accomplish and giving him the power to do it. Look how with me there is misery and with him there is mercy: so my miserable soul confides in God and calls upon the mercy of God and Peter. Therefore, misery constantly oppresses my soul which looks back at God and Peter—but will it ever see the mercy of God and Peter?

Oh God and you, the first among His Apostles: Why is my misery so immense if it is not able to be matched by the immensity of your mercy? Or, if this is in fact possible but not desirable, why is the enormity of my culpability greater than the multitude of your mercies? Maybe—just maybe—it is because I have not yet confessed all my sinfulness? But you both know that I have sinned, and this I surely confess to be true! Or is it because there is no way my confessing ever suffices? Or maybe it is that you do not repay evildoers with good? Of course, this is all true, but this is the very same misery with which I am tormented. Is it thus that the more misery seems to strangle me, the slower your mercy will come? Oh, unheard word from the merciful to the beggar!

But I do understand, just God, I do understand how you respond to my soul—that it deserves to suffer because it has willingly sinned, and that it goes unheard because of its disobedience. Alas, how bitter is my despair! I certainly acknowledge this: I acknowledge that this is a decision borne out of justice, not out of mercy. For who would call justice in my defense? My own prayer was a matter of compassion for me, not one of justice. In tribulation my suffering soul begs the bread of mercy from you, Oh God, so why do You grind the stone of justice into my mouth (cf. Lk 11:9–13)?

Let Your mercy, merciful God—through the merits and intercession of Blessed Peter, Your beloved Apostle—hasten to free my soul with its sins all forgiven. Saint Peter, prince of the Apostles, through the mercy shown you and the power bestowed upon you (Mt 18:18), break the chains of my soul and heal its wounds. Free it from the misery of sins' reign and bring it into the beatitude of the heavenly kingdom so that along with you, it can rejoice, give thanks, and worship God forever and ever, amen.

Questions for Prayerful Reflection

- Anselm sees in Peter the power of his office as shepherd, as pope. You, too, wear a Christian office—be it husband or wife, son or daughter, or perhaps it is student or even coworker, but it is ultimately the royal office of being a baptized child of your heavenly Father. Do you work to close the gap between that holy name you bear and how you conduct yourself day to day?
- St. Peter is asked by Jesus three times (Jn 21:15–17) if he loves Him so as to undo Peter's threefold denial of Jesus as Lord (Lk 22:54–62). How has Jesus offered you chances to atone for your earlier infidelities? Do you embrace current trials as such?
- Is St. Peter someone whose character and whose ministry is attractive to you? Contemplate Luke 11:9–13, one of Anselm's final biblical allusions for Peter's fatherly care. What does this tender story

tell you about God's love and how your love for your children, or the childlike in general, is a faint reflection of the Father's love for you?

Prayer to St. Stephen

St. Stephen was the first to lay his life down after the resurrection of Christ, seeing the Lord arrayed in His heavenly glory (see Acts 6–7). The Greek word "martyr" literally means to witness a significant event; to "give witness" is to attest with one's very lifeblood that what he or she is relating is true. Stephen knew the power of God, offered himself, and was ordained a deacon under the Apostles, but his fire and zeal urged him to bring the Good News to those who in no way wanted to hear it.

This prayer, number thirteen overall, is Anselm's image of heaven on earth: Stephen was so filled with the Holy Spirit that he lived a godly life to the degree of imitating Jesus all the way to the end. This is what the early Church called "red martyrdom," when Christians allow their blood to be spilled in witness to Jesus. Most Christians, however, are called to a "white martyrdom," which may not include crimson blood, but it does necessitate a day-in and a day-

out dying to self out of charity, especially when one is feeling anxious or wronged, slighted or sinned against. This type of charity may be even more difficult, for it is not achieved in the quick slash of a sword but a lifelong acceptance that all is gift and that I shall find the Lord's peace more in my stillness and silence than in my work and worldliness.

Holy Stephen, Blessed Stephen, Well-Fired Stephen,[41] strong soldier of God, first in the blessed army of God's martyrs, powerful prince, one of the great leaders in heaven, I have learned, my lord, and I have believed to hold on to this joyfully: that when you were still on earth, you radiated with such a light of sanctity, that your face shone forth with angelic dignity (Acts 6:15). You flourished with such a purity of heart that your blessed eyes looked upon God in all His glory (Acts 7:55), and you burned with such

[41] Anselm follows Christian Tradition and introduces Stephen as the Church's first martyr, thus invoking him as "benign," which comes from the Latin *bene* (good) *ignis* (flame)—to be of good fire! As one of the twelve fruits of the Holy Spirit, kindness is not simply being caring or polite, but it is to have the ardent fire of Christ Himself—the grit and determination to be virtuous always and everywhere, despite what the world might think or expect. This kind of fire is what costs Stephen and all Christian martyrs after him their life.

a sincere charity that your pious lips offered prayers for those perfidious men persecuting you (Acts 7:60).

That was the case, good Stephen, that was the case, and I rejoice it was so—and because I know this of you, I rejoice and am filled with delight, leaping for joy. I say this because I fear the strict sentence of the just Judge, that since I am a sinner and rightly deserve punishment, I have need of a helper, and I summon you as my affectionate and confident intercessor so that you may make peace with your omnipotent friend, the Lord and Creator of both me and of you.

See how the accused stands before the imposing Judge. He is indicted on many serious offenses, convicted by the witness of his own conscience as well as by the eyes of the Judge Himself. Such a man has no good deeds which can counterbalance all the evil he has done. With no real surrender in the past, he does not deserve to have a friend of the Judge act as his intercessor but deserves to be found guilty having affronted all.

The Judge is terribly relentless, intolerably severe, excessively offended, vehemently angry; and once He pronounces a sinner's sentence, it cannot be altered in any way. Open to such a one is an unending prison. In that prison, the punishments meted out are inhumane. Tormentors stand ready to seize those sentenced to damnation and drag them to their punishment: torments without end, torments without ceasing, torments without tempering—horrible punishments which never cease, which never show mercy. Fear rattles the accused, and his conscience boggles his mind, his thoughts rebuke him, and there is no way to escape. In this way, he is positioned with the severest of sentences fixed over him.

Behold this poor soul, endangered because of his suffering, suffering because of his endangerment. Behold this man in need of immediate help. But where is the help of the martyr who when weighed down by the heaviness of stones showed mercy on those who were stoning him (Acts 7:58)? When will he pray for him, praying before the harsh Judge for those who murdered him? Stephen, Stephen, truly a "*stephen*" because you have been rightly crowned.[42] Stephen, I say, Stephen, before you are a place for piety and a time for mercy, and now is your chance to exhibit charity.

---

[42] An obvious while clever wordplay: the name Stephen is derived from the Greek word for crown or wreath.

For I incessantly find myself in danger, although I am not always aware of it, and even more wretched and more miserable when I am able to ignore it. For God always sees me and my sins, His severe justice never fails to threaten the sinfulness of my soul. Hell is always open before me and God's torments are ever ready; His invisible conspirers always prepared to snatch my miserable soul away to that place. This is my state when I am awake, my state when I am asleep, when I am laughing and even when I am playing, when I am proud and when I have been brought low, when I am angry and when I have been proven right, and when I pathetically embrace fleshy delights. This is how it is for me always and everywhere. Hurry then, dutiful one, I pray: hurry before I am damned, before the hostile enemies of the human race snatch me away, before the infernal prison swallows me whole, and before the torments of Gehenna consume me.

Great are your merits, great Stephen, so, so great—able to take care of both you and me, and even if they are applied towards me, in no way are they lessened for you. Behold before God and before you, Blessed Stephen, are all my sins—those sins which abhor me, worry me, and press down upon my soul. Say, therefore, Oh pious one, say to your most affectionate and beloved Friend, "Lord, do not hold this sin against them" (Acts 7:60).

Intercede, I plead, for one so needy who asks this of you, just as you interceded for those people who put you to death. For, if this is asked in your pious charity, I am certain that the most merciful God will remit all my evil deeds. For He is merciful, and He is my Creator. I am poor and His own handiwork, while you are the beloved friend of Him Who is blessed forever and ever. Amen.

Oh, God's friend, when those maniacal enemies of His came down upon you, as the truthful Scriptures testify, you cried out in a loud voice while kneeling: "Lord, do not hold this sin against them" (Acts 7:60). Oh, your rich heart bursting with charity, from which mercy gushed forth as you were being tortured. Oh, and your mind exceedingly on fire with love, brimming with the consecrated charity, from which—when being persecuted—flashed forth flames burning sweetly and burning with sweetness. Oh honeycomb, filled with the sweet honey of love from which such opulent and joyful drops poured down when pressed upon.

"Lord, do not hold this sin against them" (Acts 7:60). Blessed man, how much hope you give to your sinful friends when they hear how you were so caring toward these unfaithful enemies of yours. You are a vessel of charity, overflowing with a fullness which you will use to slake the thirst of those willing to embrace you in their hearts, even as you poured it out upon those throwing you out of the city. For if you did so against your persecutors gasping with rage against you, how much more will you treat those who run toward you refocused and gasping with fear.

"And when he said this, he fell asleep" (Acts 7:60b). Ah, he fell asleep! Oh, sleep sweetly, sleep in safekeeping, sleep safekept in eternity. Sleep in joy, oh blessed one, and rejoice in rest. Safely you are glorified, safely in glory. Your happiness will never change, and your light will now never lessen. Whatever it was you were not able to perform because you had to be far away, you can now accomplish being near to those who pray.

For you always desire what you always have, and what has been secured for you, you always have. You certainly long for that sweet desire longingly and lusciously, always drinking with sweet passion that desire with abundant fullness. Oh, full blessedness and blessed fullness! How joyful it is to fall asleep, to fall asleep in the Lord! How peaceful they sleep, those who sleep in the Lord! The burdens of the flesh no longer weigh them down, and the hardships of the fall no longer afflict them. They no longer fight against the cravings of temptation, and being conscious of their sins no longer terrifies them.

Oh, rich and blessed peace, how far from you I stand. Behold, I crave—just a bit, to taste a drop of faraway felicity, but I am forced to choke down the bitterness of my own misery. The good things that I am not able even to imagine move me simply to be still and cry over the grave evils which in my suffering I am able to feel. Sadly, I am a miserable man—regardless of where I am, where I am not, and wherever I shall unknowingly be! My soul is dejectedly torn apart when it must interact with my flesh, unable to follow it without trepidation, but neither daring nor willing to relinquish it without travail.

I pray to you, oh blessed Stephen; I pray be compassionate to one so miserable and in need, to one who rejoices in your blessedness which cannot be diminished. Through your merits by the grace of

God through Jesus Christ our Lord, free me "from this body of this death" (Rom 7:24) so that one of these days and in the same way I too might sleep and rest in peace in the Lord, Who lives and reigns, God forever and ever. Amen.

Questions for Prayerful Reflection

- Read Acts 6, 7, and 8:1–3 and ask St. Stephen for greater insight into himself and his ministry. Imagine being in any of these scenes and ask the Holy Spirit why you are drawn here. Are you Stephen, are you one of his persecutors, or are you one of the bystanders? Let yourself sit with this moment and let come to your mind anything that speaks to you.
- Do you hold any sins against someone who has wrongly hurt you? Meditate on St. Stephen's words, "Lord, do not hold this sin against them" (Acts 7:60), and if you can, ask for the freedom to forgive those who have hurt you. What were their "stones," and why did they attack

you? Father, forgive them, they know not what they do" (Lk 23:34).

- Have you ever prayed for "a happy death"? It is a great grace to ask for now—to ask the Lord through His martyrs for the grace to have time to prepare for that last breath (the sacrament of Reconciliation), not to fear meeting Jesus, to be able to speak to your loved ones while still able, and so on (see Thomas à Kempis's Meditations on Death[43]).

Prayer to St. Paul

For St. Anselm, Paul symbolizes the life of zeal, at first a love of persecution but then, having surrendered to the Holy Spirit, a love of priestly work and prayer. This prayer is the longest of all Anselm's prayers (number ten in his collection) and taps into the point of connection Anselm shared with Paul the Apostle—awareness of personal sin and the subsequent struggle for salvation.

---

[43] The Fr. Robert Nixon translation of Thomas à Kempis's *Meditations on Death: Preparing for Eternity*, published by TAN Books in 2023, is the highest quality edition in print.

One medieval trope which might seem odd to us today is Anselm's following the Bible's lead and calling upon Christ as a loving mother (see Mt 23:37; 1 Thess 2:7; Gal 4:18–19), as that hovering caregiver who hovers over her wayward brood. This prayer opens by calling upon Paul as one abnormally born (1 Cor 15:8), as he was not one of the original twelve Apostles. Nonetheless, in Paul, Anselm finds great comfort—both came to Christ fully late in life, both have sinned greatly, and Paul's fervent remorse and understanding of the heart's entrenched iniquity are certainly Anselm's own as well.

St. Paul, you great Paul, you who are one of the great Apostles of God, and even though you came after the others, in God's vineyard you bettered them in work and impact. While still burdened by your own mortality, you were taken up "into third heaven" (2 Cor 12:2) and "taken up into Paradise" (2 Cor 12:4a), and there you heard "things not allowed to be spoken by men" (2 Cor 12:4b). Among Christians you are not only "like a nurse" (1 Thess 2:7) tending to her children, but with care and consideration you miraculously gave birth to them still again (cf. Gal 4:19). I admit that you have been made "a slave to all" (1 Cor 9:19–23) in order to "win the more" (1 Cor 9:19). By these events and through many other words and deeds, you—noble sir—are renowned throughout the world as one who is wonderfully powerful before God and immensely merciful toward your brothers and sisters. So, to you, one so great a sinner comes, one unquestionably guilty before God, the powerful and stringent Judge.

But being aware of my own conscience, I stand as my own accuser and judge. For I admit that I have sinned excessively and thus deserve perilous damnation. Even if I am not totally aware, I still see how even irrational and insensible creatures condemn me. I see how I should blush before every creature because I have sinned against Him Who alone is powerful enough to create them and Who alone is good enough to desire to have done so.[44] I am even

---

[44] Here Anselm seems to be following Augustine who in turn has received this from Plato (*Timaeus* 29D–30A). In Augustine's *Literal Commentary on Genesis*, Bk. 4.16, he argues that creation is a most fitting act because God is both *omnipotens et bonus*, both All-Powerful and All-Good. That is, the Father has both the ability to perform a generous and beautiful act and is free of envy in sharing existence, even with a metaphysically lower order of being.

damned by my own self because I was also created by Him. Sadly, when did so many and so great of evils rush in, pouring over one so miserable?

Oh, unhappy little man, what has happened to your prayer, how has your hope and trust disappeared? I had begun to pray with the assurance of bravado but then despondency set in, showing me the truth of things—namely, that my own prayer is so inadequate because of my unwillingness to trust anyone else. For if what is right stands against me, whose faithfulness could ever be with me? If all things which are good and right oppose me, whose mercy will ever come near me? If Creator and creature rightly despise me, whose face will ever shine towards me?

Oh, unhappy sinner, if this is so, nothing remains for you but an impotent hope and a silent prayer, and for you to bow down to your misery. After all, if you have made yourself so miserable, it is justly necessary that you always remain miserable.

God, Whose goodness is never extinguished, Whose mercy is never emptied, Whose knowledge never fails, Whose power achieves what it desires: How shall I ever breathe again since my sins have forced me into such a lack of hope? For if You are vengeful with sinners, kind Lord, at least grant counsel to those who seek You out. Teach me, Lord, how I ought to hope so that I am able to pray. Truly I do desire to pray to You, but I remain unaware both because of my ignorance of mind as well as my hardness of heart—both being so hindered by despair because of my iniquitousness.

I seek some excuse and ask that there is nothing to accuse me. I ask that someone pray on my behalf, but find that everything is against me. I seek for mercy on one so wretched but all that exists is against one so miserable.

Jesus, good Lord, why did You descend from heaven, and what did You accomplish in this world? Why did You hand Yourself over to death? St. Paul, while you were walking on earth, what did you teach about all this? All of God's Apostles, but especially you, invite us sinners toward faith, illustrating for us how this is our only real refuge. How could I not hope for such mercy since I believe and pray in the same faith as you? Or how could the same hope which we share thwart me since the faith which gave it birth cannot disappoint me?

Jesus, God, and you, Paul—God's apostle—because of your instruction, I—a sinner—believe in this faith, and upon this faith, I hurl myself headlong and, in fact, I have already done so. So enwrapped in this faith, I now have access to You when I go to pray. In this faith, I seek, I petition, I knock so that You might have mercy on this sinner: Jesus, You by pardoning; you, Paul, by interceding and by praying; You, God, You, by saving. Before all of You, I wrap myself up in the faith so that I might be able to hide from men who seek to measure my sins and exact their punishment, and I long to hide as well from your thrashings, God, You the demanding Judge. Because of Your reproach, a sinner asks to be hidden away, and I beg You that he is not given over by Your justice to damnation.

St. Paul, I approach you as a sinner who must be reconciled, but behold: when I near you, I am actually a dead man who must be resuscitated (see Acts 20:9–11).[45] I come as one indicted and as one in

---

[45] In Acts 20, St. Luke records a (somewhat humorous) story about a young man who, while perched on an open window ledge, fell asleep while listening to St. Paul preach. Eutyches—fittingly meaning "Good Luck"—falls three stories to his

need of an intercessor, finding that I am a corpse in need of being brought back to life. When I came to you, I was miserable but now I find I am the most miserable of all men. I approached you as one who was accused but alive, and now I find that I am both dead and damned.

So even if I have not yet been handed over to the tortuous ways of death, I have nonetheless been abandoned to that first death that leads to the next. Even if I have not yet been thrown into a prison of torment, I am nonetheless still trapped in my web of sins. Although I have not yet been lowered down into hell, I am nonetheless already dressed in the burial clothes of sin.

I was unaware and was unable to pray. This was true because I saw how deeply despicable I was to all things, and as one numb to it all, I did not grieve. Through my use of reason, I was coming to understand, but I did not grasp how death had rendered me so insensitive. Truly, I was dead and dead I approached you, and only then did I realize that I was dead.

---

death. Paul immediately quits his (obviously long) sermon and ran downstairs and threw himself on top of the boy. Certainly a good warning for clerics who tend to preach too long.

Oh God, who will pray for one so dead? St. Paul, I have brought him to you, please do not reject him.[46] Lord, Elijah and Elisha brought the dead back to life: they prostrated themselves over those corpses and transformed death into life. Lord, the living touching the dead revivified them and the dead were brought back to life for nothing but your glory. Good sir, you also said that you made yourself all things for all men (1 Cor 9:19a) so that you might win over all (1 Cor 9:19b). Friend of God, the examples of others might cause me to be impudent, but your own message only encourages my confidence. Therefore I say, lord, I say: sir, sir, come down upon me, a dead man, and stretch yourself out over this corpse, not dying yourself but becoming like the dead man (see Acts 20:10).

Therefore, St. Paul, your son has died. Mother, this dead man is certainly your son as well.[47] Sweet

---

[46] Here Anselm portrays himself carrying his old—that is, dead—self to St. Paul for intercessory healing.

[47] Here and for almost 150 more lines, Anselm follows biblical precedent and medieval custom by invoking both St. Paul as well as Jesus Christ as "Mother," highlighting their compassion and caregiving. We have already encountered the New Testament imagery of mother hen and nurse, but there is also rich

mother, acknowledge your son by the voice of his pleading, as he acknowledges his own mother through the sweetness of her compassion. Acknowledge your son by the confession of his Christian faith, as he acknowledges his own mother through the sweetness of her piety. Mother, offer to grant new birth to your sons and daughters, offer your dead son to be resuscitated yet again by the One Who gives new life to His servants through His own death.

Oh mother, offer your guilty children who deserved death to the One Who died undeservedly. Offer your son up to Him so He can call him back to new life. Through baptism, this son of yours was rescued from death, but through meaninglessness and depravity, he has been led back into death. Oh, mother, renowned for your affection, your child feels deeply the warmth of your maternal love. Present him to that One Who has also revived you and Who preserved you while living. Pray to God for

---

Old Testament usage of maternal qualities for God (e.g., Dt 32:11; Ps 131:1–2; Is 49:15; 66:13). Even in his *Life of St. Anselm*, Eadmer refers to Anselm as "a father to the healthy and a mother to the sickly" (*Vita Sancti Anselmi* I.xiii).

your son because he is His servant; pray to God for His servant because he is your son.

But you, Jesus, good Lord, are you also not my mother? Are You not a mother, the mother hen who gathers her brood beneath her wings (Lk 13:34)? Truly, Lord, You are my mother. For those who give birth as well as those who are born are received by You. You were the first to die, and in dying they have been born.[48] For unless You had given birth, You would not have undergone death; and unless You had died, You would have not given birth.[49] Desiring to birth sons and daughters into life, You savored death, and while dying, You brought them forth. You did this through Your own Self, while those whom You command and aid, they must do it through You—You as the Author, they as Your coworkers. Therefore, Lord God, You are the great Mother.

---

[48] The "first" to die here (*prius*) is of course not a chronological or a temporal statement but a metaphysical or even theological one: Jesus is the first to die in that in His death all other souls are gathered and offered the freedom of being reborn unto eternal life.

[49] Perhaps Anselm has John 3 in mind here where Jesus and Nicodemus picture true life in terms of dying and being reborn.

In this way, You and St. Paul are both my mothers. Even if you are also fathers, you are still mothers. For you have made it so that those born to death should be reborn to life: You, Jesus, on Your own power, while you, Paul, rebirth through Jesus's power. You are both fathers because of your effect, mothers because of your affect. Fathers through authority, mothers through kindness. Fathers through instruction, mothers through mercy. You, Jesus, are therefore a mother, and you as well, Paul. And even though you two are unequal in the amount of affection you possess, your affection is not unlike in its essence. Although you might not be matched in the magnitude of your kindness, you agree wholeheartedly in your will. While not equals in your plenitude of mercy, you are not wholly unequal in your intentions.

Mother Christ, You who gather Your chickens under your wings (see Lk 13:34), this moribund chicken of Yours now places himself under Your wings. By Your tenderness the terror-stricken are consoled, by Your scent the desperate are brought to. Your warmth vivifies the dead, while Your nearness saves sinners. Know, my mother, Your dead son—know him by both the sign of Your Cross and the voice of his confession. Warm up Your chick, resuscitate Your dead son, save Your sinner. May Your terror-stricken son be consoled by You; desperate in himself, may he be consoled by You and may he be born again through Your unbroken and unending grace. You flood sinners with consolation, and so may You be blessed forever and ever. Amen.

Questions for Prayerful Reflection

- How have you tried to become "all things to all people"—at work, at home, in the community? Do you pray to see how Christ might use you to evangelize and to interact with others where they are at and neither dismiss them nor talk above them?
- Does the more maternal imagery for Jesus or St. Paul here help or hinder your prayer? Can you understand its appeal to Anselm—a person who is quintessentially (if not stereotypically) nurturing, loving, sympathetic?
- Paul is known for his great conversion. Read Acts 9 and see what moment of Paul's early encounter with Christ most

resonates with you. What might the Holy Spirit be trying to tell you as you reflect on the life of this great apostle? Paul also left us thirteen epistles in the New Testament—you might read one of those straight through as you come to know this powerful convert. How do you want St. Paul to pray for you right now?

Prayer to St. Benedict

Having begun his religious life as a Benedictine oblate, brother, and eventually chosen to go on toward priesthood, Anselm's studies and spirituality centered around the life of St. Benedict—his example and writings, his vision for holiness, and—more practically—the way of life he had set up almost half a century before Anselm shadowed the doors of the Monastery of Bec.

St. Benedict of Nursia (d. 550) wrote his Rule around 530 and stands as the first in the West to amass and modify the ancient teachings of the Desert Fathers. For after the legalization of Christianity by Emperor Constantine in 313, the monk replaced the martyr as the Christian hero; and towering figures like St. Anthony the Great (d. 356) provided direction for hermits (from the Greek word for "desert"), St. Pachomius (d. 348) devised the first guide for cenobitic dwellings ("from living together"—koinonia, "common" and bios "life"), while women like St. Melania the Elder established a woman's community in Jerusalem in 379. This prayer (numbered fifteen by Anslem) thanks Benedict for his vision, praises him for his virtue, and pleads for his gracious understanding for the disparity between the ideal of the monk Benedict wants and the sinful state Anselm finds himself.

Holy and blessed Benedict, heavenly grace has made you rich with an overflowing blessing of the virtues. All this has been granted not only so that you would be raised to your desired glory, brought to blessed peace and to a heavenly throne, but so that innumerable others could also be attracted to that same blessedness—those who are in awe of your life, moved by your kindly admonitions, instructed by your tender teachings, and called forth through your miracles.

Blessed of God, whom God has blessed with many blessings, my anguished soul takes refuge in you. With as much of a humble mind as possible, I cast myself down before you; with as much affection as possible, my prayers flood before you; and with as much longing as possible, I beg your help, for my need is too great, my need is too intolerable.

I have professed a life to be reformed constantly in holiness, promising the name and the habit of a monk.[50] However, my long life has cast me far from this, and my conscience convicts me to admit that I have lived as a fake before God, His angels, and all mankind. Be present, loving Father Benedict, be present to the one who cries out to you. I pray that you are not horrified by so many lies and so much deceit, but that it might please you to attend to what I have to confess and to have more mercy on my agony than I deserve.

You are, of course, the illustrious leader among the great armies of Christ, having led me to serve

---

[50] When Anselm professed vows as a Benedictine, he would have promised the evangelical counsels of chastity, poverty, and obedience but he would also have promised stability—not to seek other missions and monasteries—and "*conversation morum,*" or a constant spirituality of conversion of soul. This uniquely monastic vow encompassed both a spiritual battle of always choosing to grow in holiness as well the more mundane promises of living by the daily schedule, contributing to the needed work of the monastery, and all the other challenges communal living necessarily entails.

under your command, although I am such a stumbling soldier and such a stupid student. Yet I have vowed to live according to your *Rule*, however lecherous a monk I have been. For my deviant heart is as cold and dry as any stone when it comes to regretting all the sins I have committed.

Yet when it comes to resisting those occasions of sin, my heart is all too accommodating and soon defiled. My depraved mind eagerly and constantly dwells on useless and vile things. Even to consider what is good tires my brain and renders it thoughtless.

My blinded and distorted soul is all too keen and undemanding and so it hurls itself into sins and just wallows there. But how it resists and how sluggish it is when bringing the virtues to mind. Dearest Father Benedict, it is too long of a tale to recall each and every time this has happened. I admit that it would take too long to enumerate all the gluttony, spiritual sloth, flippancy, impatience, vainglory, detraction, disobedience, and all the other vices which my sad soul commits, making of me a constant mockery.[51]

---

[51] Anselm once again uses a version of the traditional listing of the deadly sins in which to see his own soul; for more on the

At times these sins toss me here and there, simply toying with me, an uncaring and ragged little man. At other times these sins insult me by stomping on me, and they stomp on me by insulting me.

Behold, Blessed Benedict, how eagerly this soldier of Christ wages war under your banner. Behold how this disciple of yours, in your school, advances: behold a good monk who mortifies his sins and carnal pleasures of life, fervent and lives only for the virtues. But no, you see only a monk who is a fake, one who stifles all virtue, is overwhelmed by a vulgar herd of vices, and who is weighed down by a mountain of sins.

What shame! Oh, what a shameless monk. What audacity for me to call myself a soldier of Christ, a follower of St. Benedict! You're a poser in your profession, and what insolence to be seen in the tonsure and clothed in the cowl when you don't live that life. Oh, what pain, what "anguish that closes in on every side" (2 Cor 4:8). If I deny my highest King, my good teacher, along with my vowed vocation, my lot

---

deadly sins, see the first prayer to Mother Mary above where she proves to be an antidote against acedia.

is death.[52] However, even if I can *profess* myself to be a soldier, a scholar, as well as a monk, *my way of life* insists that I am actually a liar, and my lot is judgment. Oh, my soul, you should be troubled, and my heart should be disturbed, so break free and cry out!

Jesus, good Lord, "Look upon my affliction and suffering; take away all my sins" (Ps 25:18). "Be my helper," Lord, "do not cast me off; do not forsake me" (Ps. 27:9), but "Teach me to do Your will" (Ps 143:10) so that my life might give witness to what my heart and my mouth confess so willingly. "Attend to the sound of my cry, my King and my God!" (Ps 5:3), through the merits and the intercession of loving Benedict, Your beloved, my Commander and my Teacher.

Oh, you, my good superior, my tender teacher, oh sweet Father Benedict: I pray, I beg you through the mercy you have had for so many others, and through the mercy that God has had for you, be compassionate to me in my misery, for I rejoice with you in your blessedness.

---

52 Here Anselm sees his eternal life in terms of three fonts of saving grace: his relationship with Jesus, his obedience to the Benedictine life, and the vows he has undertaken in his religious life.

Grant me succor as I call out to you as my patron. Help rescue me from the mountain of sins that smothers my soul, unravel the knots of sin which now bind me, and disentangle me from the crimes that strangle me. Raise me when cast down, strengthen me when unsteady, instruct the helpless with the spiritual arms of holiness, teach and protect the warrior and "war upon those who make war upon me" (Ps 35:10).

Please do this, you who intercede for monks; do it for the sake of that charity which you were so eager for us to profess as a way of life. Do this so that we may truly desire and effectively achieve what we should in whatever way possible, so that both you—because of our discipleship—and we—because of your leadership—may shine in glory in the presence of God, who lives and reigns forever and ever. Amen.

Questions for Prayerful Reflection

- Let us not think of Anselm the Monk as someone special and so set apart that his daily demands are not ours as well. You, too, have a vow of obedience, as your baptism and following Christ makes demands on how you can live, what you can say, and what you call "real." Regardless of your state in life, you, too, are called to be chaste and never to reduce another or yourself to an object of sexual pleasure. You, too, are called to faithful financial stewardship and, ultimately, to be "poor in spirit," in that you are ever grateful for having received all the goods of this life and to use them as Jesus asks.

- Does Anselm's admittance that he is not living his monastic life to the full cause any guilt in you for not living as a Christian in the world 24/7? Where do you feel challenged imagining Jesus asking what you have done for Him lately? Today?
- Read the *Rule of St. Benedict*[53] and spend time with this ancient wisdom and see where the life of a sixth-century monk and yours today overlap.

[53] St. Benedict of Nursia, *The Rule of St. Benedict* (Gastonia, NC: TAN Books, 2018).

IV.

Prayers and Meditations for the Church Militant

Included here are Anselm's prayers for his friends, for his enemies, and two of his later meditations. These all share the archbishop's desire to care for people still on earth. No one individual is named, making these prayers as inclusive as possible: those lovingly close to those who pray, those who have betrayed us, a meditation on our own lost fidelity, and one on what it means to be redeemed in Jesus Christ.

A Prayer for My Friends

Anselm's letters are full of themes involved in friendship, a bond he takes very seriously. For it is Jesus Himself Who calls us friends, and this invitation elevates each of us into a divine union. The prayer, therefore, is not that Jesus could love us more but that we become more trusting to open ourselves up to Him and His Love. This is daunting in that staying aloof is simply much easier—no one cares, no one checks up on us, no one is asking questions we do not want to answer, and so on. The mercy Anselm asks for here in prayer number seventeen is to transform us from secretly desiring to stay apart from Jesus into His confidants and friends, thus cementing all our human friendships as well.

Sweet and tender Lord Jesus Christ, You Who showed love greater than anyone, a love no one has ever matched, in no way deserved to die, but You still laid down Your life for both Your servants as well as for sinners, even praying for them as they were crucifying You.

You wanted to make these men Your brothers, to justify them and so reconcile them to Your merciful Father and to Yourself. You, Lord, Who showed such great charity to Your enemies, also showed this same love to Your friends.

Good Lord, with what depth could I ever recall Your immeasurable love? How could I ever repay You for such an immense gift? For the sweetness of Your kindness transcends every feeling. The greatness of Your goodness outruns any return. How could I ever repay my Creator and Recreator? Lord, "You are my

God" (Ps 16:2a), "You certainly do not need any of my 'goods'" (Ps 16:2b).[54] For the entire earth and all that fills it is Yours.

Therefore, how could I who am a beggar, a man who is destitute, mere vermin and ashes, repay my God unless I follow His teachings from my heart? For this is Your commandment: that we "love one another" (Jn 13:34). Good Man, Good God, Good Lord, Good Friend, You are the good in whatever is, and Your humble and wretched servant longs to obey Your command. You know, Lord, how I love the love which You command, holding this love dear and longing for this charity.

This I seek, this I ask, and to obtain it, Your poor and needy beggar knocks and cries out at the door of Your mercy (Mt 7:7–8). And now that I have already received the sweet almsdeeds of Your undeserved

---

[54] The wording of Anselm's Bible here reads a bit differently than our modern versions today, but the point of Psalm 16:2 is the same: God is the true Good, Goodness Itself, and all other creatures are good because they share in God for all they are and do. Yet there are imposters of the good—ersatz substitutes that we may call "good" but really are not—and these Anselm is discerning in his life so as not to offer these simulacra of the Good back to God.

bounty, loving all people in You and because of You (see Mt 22:36–40), although neither as much as I should nor as I would really like, though I plead for Your mercy on all peoples.

Accordingly, there are many more whom I love more dearly because Your Love has impressed them more familiarly upon my heart, and desiring their love more ardently, I pray more devoutly for them. But Your servant desires—he desires, Holy Lord—to pray to You for these friends, but I am guilty and thus confined by my sins. And if I am unable to achieve my own forgiveness, can I really presume to be so bold and ask Your forgiveness for others?

Furthermore, I so anxiously ask others to prayerfully intercede for me, how can I be so bold to presume to pray on behalf of others? What shall I do, Lord God, what shall I do? You command me to pray for them and my heart desires to do so, but my conscience cries out against me, telling me that I should care more about my own sins, and so fear to speak on behalf of others.

So, does that mean I should put aside what You command because I have done something You have prohibited? No. Rather, because I have already undertaken what is forbidden, I shall embrace what You ask, trusting that my obedience may heal my presumption and charity cover the multitude of my sins (1 Pt 4:8).

I therefore pray to You, holy and good God, for those who love me because of You and those whom I love in You: for those You see who love me more devoutly and those whom I love more sincerely. But I am not doing this, my Lord, as someone who is virtuous and safe from sins but as one who is concerned about loving even strangers. Love them, You Who are the Source of Love, and You Who provide the command (cf. Jn 13:34a) and the source (cf. Jn 13:34b) by which I too might love them.

And if my prayer does not achieve any advantage for them because it is offered up by one so sinful, let it be of value to them since it is offered because You have commanded so. On account of You, Author and Bestower of charity, on account of Who You are and not for my sake, love them and make them love You with all of their heart, all of their mind, and all of their soul (Mt 22:37) so that they will desire, say, and do only what is pleasing to You and thus salvific for them.

Too cold, too cold is my prayer, my Lord, because my charity burns so slightly. But You Who are so rich in mercy will not measure out Your graciousness to my friends according to the dullness of my devotion. Rather, since Your kindness surpasses all human love, let Your longing to hear our prayers transcend the reverence of my prayer. Do this for them and on account of their needs, Lord, hearing their prayers so that it assists them according to your will. Only then can they be ruled and protected by You forever and everywhere, thereby reaching Your glorious and eternal security, You Who live and reign, God forever and ever. Amen.

Questions for Prayerful Reflection

- With whom do you feel closest in this world? Who are your closest friends? What are their characteristics that most draw you?
- Do you see in your best friend someone you wish you were more like? In the soul of the one closest to us are qualities we not only admire but also desire to acquire

for ourselves. Do you feel this to be true?

❧ Very practically speaking, do you keep a list of names of people for whom you pray daily? Could you begin to form such a list and keep it in the prayer book or Bible you most consistently use?

A Prayer for My Enemies

This prayer is "real" (numbered nineteen in Anselm's collection) in that we all have past hurts and people whom we might consider enemies or who consider us to be so. Jesus works to give us the supernatural grace of charity which allows us to love our enemies; this shows that love is not simply natural or only human. Love, as we have seen, is God's very nature and that is the gift He gives us through the Holy Spirit: "the love of God has been poured out into our hearts through the Holy Spirit that has been given to us" (Rom 5:5).

Most powerful and holy Lord Jesus Christ, Whom I beg to be gracious to all of my friends, You know my heart and what it wants for my enemies. For You are "God who tries hearts and minds" (Ps 7:10), penetrating my soul's innermost secrets. All things lie open to You, and if You have sown anything in the soul of Your servant that can be offered up to You, it cannot be concealed from you. But if my enemy, the enemy of human nature, has planted anything else there (cf. Mt 13:28), let it be burned up by Your fire (cf. Mt 13:30).

Do not forsake, most gracious God, that which You have planted, but nurture, increase, perfect, and keep it. For I am not able to do any good deed without You (cf. Jn 15:5), nor am I able to keep or complete anything without You. Merciful God, please do not judge me according to what is displeasing within me but root out anything which You did not put there (cf. Lk 19:21), saving this soul which You have created.

Without You, I could never correct myself because You alone created what is good in us.[55] My soul could not survive if You chose to judge it according to its sinfulness (Ps 130:3).

---

[55] This reflects St. Augustine's great insight that the only thing he can call wholly his own are his sins: "Your justice alone sets me free, nothing but my sins can I call my own" (*Expositions of the Psalms*, *en. Ps.* 70, *exp.* 1.20).

You, Lord, alone are power; You alone are mercy. Whatever desires for my enemies You Yourself place within me, grant that to them and repay me with the same. Good Lord, if I ever ask for anything which falls outside what is charitable—whether through my own stupidity, infirmity, or malice—do not grant that to them nor pay it back to me.

You Who are true Light, illumine their darkness. You are the ultimate Truth; put right their errors. For You have said to Your beloved disciple, "Whoever does not love remains in death" (1 Jn 3:14). I therefore beg You, Lord, that you will give to them a love for both their neighbor as well as for You, insofar as You desire this, and so that they should not sin against their brother in your sight.

Oh loving Lord, do not allow me to be an occasion of death for others, lest I become for them a scandalous stone (1 Pt 2:8) and a rock of offense.[56] It is surely more than enough that I am a scandal to myself, Lord, and my own sin is certainly sufficient. Your servant implores You on behalf of his

[56] The biblical word for "scandal" literally means that which trips another up (See the *Catechism of the Catholic Church* §2284).

arrange this same penance for me, as one who sins against You, as well.

Come then, good Creator, my Merciful Judge, and through Your mercy which is greater than any anger, forgive me all my sins as I stand before You, and forgive all those who have sinned against me (Mt 6:12; Lk 11:4). And although I have not yet forgiven my enemies as perfectly as You would, my soul does desire to do so, and so I am using all my might to forgive through You. I thus offer to You what I can so that you might forgive my sins perfectly and treat me as graciously as You can.

Hear me, hear, Oh great Lord, good Lord, for my soul longs and hungers to feast upon the warmth of Your love. Yet my soul is unable to satisfy itself with You. For my mouth finds no name to invoke which can satisfy my heart, and none of my own words satisfy my taste when my affections receive from You whatever it is You give. Lord, I have prayed as I am able, but my desire is greater than my ability. So hear, hear me as You are able, because You can do whatever You will. I have prayed as one who is weak and sinful; hearken and hear me as One Who is all-powerful and all-merciful.

Bring this prayer to completion, not only for my friends but also for my enemies whom I now hold in prayer. Yet pour out the remedy of Your mercy on all the living and the dead, wherever it is according to Your will and wherever it will save others. Hear me not according to what my heart seeks nor what my mouth says, but always hear me according to what You know and want me to desire and wish for, Oh Savior of the world, Who lives and reigns with the Father and the Holy Spirit, God forever and ever. Amen.

Questions for Prayerful Reflection

- What enemies have you encountered in your life's story? Are you able in earnest to pray for these people's eternal well-being? Who might consider you an enemy?
- Do you see how true love (cf. 1 Cor 13) is synonymous with God's very Self and not just a feeling we conjure when things are going well? Loving one's enemies and those whom we might not naturally like is proof that love is from God. Where

have you experienced this? Where do you desire to experience it?

- Do you understand Anselm's constant insistence that our desires are dearer to God than our words? None of us are articulate enough to impress the heavenly realm, but God sees our heart's deepest wants. Is this of comfort to you or does this increase your anxiety? When it comes to a life and an eternity, what is it you really desire?

Sorrow for a Virginity Wrongly Wasted

There are various ways to interpret this prayer for one still alive. The lost virginity St. Anselm so passionately weeps over could be a callow dalliance of his youth but, perhaps more likely, is a spiritual metaphor for a heart torn between love of God and love of self. In the Christian tradition, virginity can simply mean the state of sexually abstaining, but it can also refer to the spiritual state of loving God with an undivided heart, a state of soul wherein the disciple is wholeheartedly committed to the Lord and to no one or nothing else.

fellow servants: do not allow me to be the cause of their offense against the favor of so great and loving Lord. Instead, allow them to be reconciled to you and harmoniously together let us live in accord with Your will simply for Who You are.

In the hidden places of my heart, I hold a vindication which I hope to see carried out for both those who labor alongside me as well as for those who sin along with me. Again, this is the "punishment" that my soul seeks, for those who serve You with me as well as for those still my enemies: that we might love You and love one another as you desire (Mt 22:37–39), as this would be nothing other than our saving grace.[57] Then we can atone for our own sins as well as for how each of us has sinned against the gracious Lord so that together we may begin to follow in charity the one Lord and Master. This is the chastening Your sinful servant asks to be meted out to all who desire my downfall and act to bring about my sorrow. Too, perfectly merciful Lord,

[57] Anyone who moves from darkness into light realizes that what they once considered a punishment (e.g., daily discipline, a healthy lifestyle, the practice of Christian prayer and charity, etc.) actually see it as their "saving grace" once they have been freed from wrong opinion and their selfish habits.

Here in Anselm's second meditation, the focus is on asking the Holy Spirit for greater clarity in how often we turn away from what is Good and True and instead settle for lesser goods and truth only when convenient. This is what Anselm means by "fornication"—the willingness to be comfortable with what is in reality uncomfortable.

My soul, my miserable soul, I'm speaking to you, the soul of a miserable little man: Throw off your torpor, get rid of your sinfulness, and clear your mind. Bring back to your heart an immense offense and from that heart let out a huge roar: hear, you sad soul, the horror of your sinfulness; hold your horrible terror up before you, and gaze, too, upon your terrific sorrow. For you were once a virgin, a spouse of Christ, having been washed with a celestial purity, having been given over to the Holy Spirit and freely professing the Christian Faith.

Oh, how I remember back then! How I have named it! But now Jesus is no longer the kindly spouse of my virginity but the terrifying Judge of my infidelity. Alas, with the memory of joys now abandoned, why is the weight of my current unhappiness even more unbearable? How miserable is the lot of the wicked, tormented equally by anything—bad or good! An evil and tortured conscience torments me and I fear it will consume me. Even my good conscience mocks me, for the memory of the rewards of virtue I know I have lost and can never again have back. Oh, what a misery to forego what is so painful to lose—to lose irretrievably what ought to have been preserved forever! Oh, what an inconsolable loss—not only the destruction of what has been good but the receiving of what is torturous!

Oh Virginity, once you were my delight but now you are my loss and my despair. Where have you fled to, into what filth and in what bitter vileness have you abandoned me? Oh, fornication, you are the degeneracy of my mind and the destroyer of my soul—how you have snuck up on me in my misery and from such a bright and pleasant place hurled me down headlong. Fornication is a bitter woe, one that has consumed me and one that has misspent my gift of virginity. This is a wounding pain and what's even more painful than this loss is that it was replaced by fornication. For the first is an irreplaceable failure, while the latter is an intolerable torment. Misery on this side and on that side. So, again, equally both good and evil exact justice and both punish me miserably while I live. Justifiably and deservedly, indeed.

Oh my soul, you are so unfaithful to God, you have broken your oath to God, an adulterer to Christ, you have freely fled the grandeur of virginity and are now miserably plunged into the infernal regions of fornication. Once you were espoused to the King of heaven, but you have now eagerly made yourself the courtesan of hell's tyrant. Ah, a soul who has disassociated itself from God and has dashed toward the devil. You wretch, you are my greatest misery, an obstinate whore and a shameless fornicator: you felt free enough to offer a bill of divorce to God, your first Lover and Creator, God, and instead freely handed yourself over to the devil who will prove to be your destroyer and murderer.

What a most miserable exchange, ha, it's even worse than "miserable." Oh, what a sublime height you have fallen from and into what a pit have you been plunged. Alas, you have grown to hate tenderness and have instead united yourself to iniquity. What have you done, my demented mind? What have you done, now that you are mindless of impurity, mindless of filthy wickedness? You have abandoned your

Chaste Lover in heaven and have instead pursued your hateful corrupter into hell, preparing in that abyss not a lovely marital bed but your own brothel. What an astounding horror that your will is so perverted. What a horrible marvel that your perversity is so voluntary! Oh, God, where am I able to find a remedy for such a perversity? Where, Oh God, shall I ever get satisfaction for such a crime?

You might as well hurl yourself into the deep darkness of unbounded sorrow, you miserable little man, since you have already fallen into the hell of horrible wickedness. You sad soul, submerge yourself into some terrible mass of pain since you have already fallen willingly into the stinking mire of hell. Wrap yourself up in agony, in a horrible darkness of inconsolable grief, since you have already freely rolled around in the void of such sordid luxury. Wallow in the babbling of bitterness since you have already wallowed in the trough of moral decay.

Horrible terror, terrible horror, an inconsolable grief, pile yourself upon me. It's right, it's right that you rush over me, overwhelm me, disturb me, envelop and possess me. I despised you with brazen nerve, and with impudent pleasure I provoked you.

But even more did I provoke God and not you, and now I long for you with a pitiful repentance. Torment the sinner and vindicate God: allow the hellish fornicator to suffer the tortures he now deserves, let him have a foretaste of what he has prepared for himself, and let him get used to what he is about to suffer. Unconscionable sinner, unfurl and bring about your mournful repentance, you who have yielded to the impurity of your sinfulness for way too long. Grow dizzy and dizzy as you spin in the whirlpool of your sins, just as you have been rolling around so much in the dizziness of lasciviousness.

I no longer want consolation, security, and joy, I repeat, I do not want you unless being forgiven of my sins brings you back to me. If you are far from me before I die, then maybe mercy will recall you back to me after I die. Let unending penance become the bitter penance of my life; let seething pain become the insatiable persecutor of my life; allow sadness and bitter sorrows be the tireless tormentors of my youth as well as my old age.

Oh, if only this were the case, if only so! I hope, I pray, I long that it be so. For I am no longer worthy to raise my eyes to heaven in prayer, but I am not so unworthy that I cannot blind them with tears. If my mind is too confounded with shame to pray, let it be equally disturbed with a mournful whirlwind of grief and sorrow. If it is too frightening to appear before the face of God, then it is right that I should have to live before the face of my sin's torments.

My heart thus thinks about—and even dwells on—what it did and what it deserves. So, let my heart descend deeper, let it descend I say, "into the land of darkness and into the shadows of death" (Job 10:21), and let it consider what awaits my sinful soul there. Let me concentrate and contemplate, let my mind see and be disturbed: What God, what is this that I can foresee, this land of "misery and darkness" (Job 10:22a)? Horror, horror! What is this I heed, where one must live "with no order but only everlasting horror" (Job 10:22b)? Oh my, what a confusing din, what a tumult of gnashing teeth, what a chaotic clamor of screaming. Sadly, sadly, how much and how much sorrow. Sulfurous flame, the flames of the underworld, swirling with terrible screams from the smoke.

Vermin living in that fire, is it not a wonder that your tendency to gnaw away should not consume you and you get burned up in the fiery flame? Demons furious with fire, gnashing your teeth in anger, why are you so merciless to those who are writhing in pain among you? Is every torment moderated by justice but endless in terms of punishment—no moderation, no respite, no end which could ever subdue you? Are these punishments the end, Great God? Is this what has been prepared for all those who fornicate against You and hold Your ways in contempt, among whom I am now counted?[58]

I am now one of them. Me! So, my soul, tremble in fear; my mind, shrivel up; my heart, be rendered. And you who carry out the sentence of my crime, where are you dragging me? And you, my sinfulness, where are you driving me? And you, my God,

[58] Anselm tries to sync souls writing in eternal pain with the love of God, the first major theme Dante Alighieri (d. 1321) will illuminate relatively soon hereafter. In short, God "sends" to hell only the souls who choose to go there and that is how hell is a matter of justice and not revenge or hatred. Approaching the gates into hell, Dante wonders how such a structure could be of God and there he reads the gates telling him, "Sacred Justice moved my Architect. I was raised by divine Omnipotence, primordial Love and ultimate Intellect." From *The Divine Comedy, Inferno*, Canto 3, lines 4–6; trans., John Ciardi (Berkley: New York City, 2003), 31.

to where are You relinquishing me? If I have done that which renders me Your prisoner, surely I am not able to be so evil that I am no longer Your creature? Even though I have stolen away my chastity, surely You cannot take away Your mercy? Lord, O Lord, I have acted in such a way that deserves condemnation, but certainly You have not grown unaccustomed to saving? Refuse, Lord, refuse to treat my evil in such a way that You forget your own goodness. Oh where, most Truthful God, is it found, "I do not will the death of a sinner but that he turn from his wicked way and live" (Ez 18:32, 33:11)? So, Lord, if You cannot lie (Heb 6:18)—You, Lord, Who "does not desire the death of sinners"—would it be right if You buried in hell a sinner now crying out to You?

Is plunging a sinner into Gehenna "desiring not the death of a sinner"? Is this not rather, "I desire that a sinner convert and so live" (Ez 33:11)? I am that sinner, Lord, I am that sinner! Thus, if You do not desire the death of a sinner, what compels You against Your will, that You would hand me over to death? But if You so desire that a sinner convert his ways and live, what prohibits You from doing what

You desire—namely, converting me so I might live? Does the enormity of my sinfulness force You to do what You do not will to do, even though you are the Omnipotent God? No way, my God, no way, my Lord: let not the sinfulness of a grieving sinner confessing to You overrule the will of the Almighty.

Remember, Just and Kindly God, remember that You are merciful, both my Creator and my Restorer. Good Lord, do not conjure up Your justice against Your sinner, but remember that You are tender with your creature. Do not recall Your anger against Your accused, but remember You are merciful with the merciless. It is true that my conscience deserves damnation and that no penance of mine could ever make proper satisfaction, but what is certain is that your mercy prevails over every possible offense.[59]

---

[59] Satisfaction is Anselm's core theological tenet. He realizes no fallen child of Adam can ever "satisfy" or atone for humanity's sinfulness, and so he must rely fully and entirely on the man Who is also God, Jesus Christ. It is in Him that all these prayers and meditations must occur, as no sinful soul can approach the Father without a Mediator and in Christ's sacred humanity all find who they too can become, and that alone can soothe the conscience.

Spare me then, Good Lord, You to Whom salvation belongs and Who does not desire the death of a sinner, spare my sinful soul. Out of terror my soul flees Your terrifying justice and seeks refuge in Your comforting mercy. But since the prize of my corrupted virginity is now—oh, the pain—irrecoverable, at least may the punishment of this fornicator who now confesses to You be neither inevitable nor impossible for Your omnipotence, may it be neither unfitting for Your justice, nor unusual for Your mercy—for You are Good (1 Chr 16:34a) and Your mercy is everlasting (1 Chr 16:34b), You Who are blessed forever and ever. Amen.

Questions for Prayerful Reflection

- Does the word "virginity" evoke images of purity of heart or prudishness for you today? Do you see how you can understand virginity in terms of purity of heart, single-heartedness, and undistracted focus, and not only sexually? What would it mean for you to embrace such a spirituality, to pray to be more single-minded in your union with Jesus?

- Do your sins seem unrelenting and merciless, as Anselm prays here? What most nags at you and causes your soul the most anxiety? Such badgering is usually from the enemy and not from the Holy Spirit, who longs to soothe your soul and inspire in you thoughts of perseverance, fidelity, and joy. List what most bothers you and pray over that feeling or fear, and let the Holy Spirit offer you calm.
- Do you ever feel you "deserve" God's condemnation? That is not from God, for He has claimed you in baptism and has fed you your entire life, eucharistically as well as existentially! Pray to be freed from any consternation over your salvation but realize that this is a gift, and while it can never be presumed, a Christian soul should trust in the promise of Christ that He loves you and wants to bring you forever into His own Self. Pray over all the ways Jesus shows you His care—you may want to jot down all these blessings and pray in gratitude over each.

Meditation on Human Redemption

We are all easily deceived. We are willingly fooled not because we are ignorant (most of the time) but because we want to be. For instance, there are times when we want to believe how extra dessert is really good for us, how this "little" lie or pilfering of a pen or some small item doesn't really hurt anyone, that my own uncharitable or lustful thoughts don't really affect me. The Truth cannot deceive although we are all able to make it so. In his third meditation, Anselm reflects on how the heart of Christianity is found in the Cross, in the lowliness of a God made flesh. We, however, tend to run from this truth and instead limit God to the ceremonial and the pristine, while He is more likely found in the destitute and downtrodden.

Christian soul, a soul resurrected from cruel death, a soul redeemed and freed from miserable enslavement by God's own blood, awaken your mind and recall how you have been resurrected. Recognize your redemption and liberation. Recall the source and the strength of your salvation; enter its meditation and delight in its contemplation. Throw off your indifference, strengthen your heart, and focus your mind. Taste the goodness of your salvation and enkindle in your heart a love of your Savior. Bite down upon His words as a honeycomb, savor their tastiness sweeter than honey, and then swallow that life-giving goodness: bite by thinking, suck by contemplating, and swallow by loving and rejoicing. Exult in your biting, be grateful in your sucking, and delight in your swallowing.[60]

So, what is the source and strength of your salvation? Certainly, it is Christ Who has resurrected you. He is the Good Samaritan Who has healed you (cf. Lk 10:33–35), that trustworthy Friend (cf. Jn 15:15) Who has redeemed and released you from bondage; it is Christ, I say! Therefore, the strength of your salvation is nothing other than the strength of Christ.

---

[60] Referring to the study of Scripture as eating, Anselm plays off a very biblical metaphor—to consume the Word of God, a foreshadowing of the Eucharist. Think of how the prophet Ezekiel is told, "Son of man, eat what you find here: eat this scroll, then go, speak to the house of Israel" (Ez 3:1). Too, John relates how sweet this Word ultimately is: "So I went up to the angel and told him to give me the small scroll. He said to me, 'Take and swallow it. It will turn your stomach sour, but in your mouth it will taste as sweet as honey'" (Rv 10:9).

But what is the source of Christ's strength? For sure, "Horns are in his hands, because his hands have been nailed to the arms of the Cross" (Hab 3:4). But how can there be strength in such weakness? What depth can there be in this lowliness? What is to be admired in such contempt? There is something certainly hidden in this infirmity, concealed in this humility, something mysterious in this contempt. Oh, what hidden strength: by hanging from a Cross, a man can lift the weight of unending death from the human race; a man nailed to a tree can loosen the bonds of eternal death which ensnare this world.

Oh what hidden power: a man condemned to die alongside thieves saves all men condemned along with demons (cf. Mt 27:38; Mk 15:27; Lk 23:33); a man stretched out on the Cross draws all things to Himself (Jn 12:32)! Oh, secret strength: one Soul sent into torment draws innumerable souls from those flames; a man suffers the death of His body and so defeats the death of souls.

Good Lord, loving Redeemer, powerful Savior, why did You choose to work such strength under such lowliness? Did You do this to trick the devil who, by tricking man, ejected him from paradise?[61] But the truth can never deceive anyone. For whoever is ignorant or who refuses to assent to the truth only deceives himself. Whoever sees the truth and either hates or disregards the truth only deceives himself. The truth deceives no one.

But could it have been the case that the devil deceived himself? Just as the truth never deceives anyone, neither does it ever intend to make someone deceive himself (although it might be accused of doing so when "the truth" allows it). For You assumed human nature not to hide what was already known about Yourself but to manifest what was not yet known. You have told us and by Your actions

---

[61] Tricking the devil has a long history in the Church's theology. Ignatius of Antioch (d. 107) argued that Mary's virginity was "kept secret from this world's prince" (*Epistle to the Ephesians* §19), while later Church Fathers represented the Crucified Christ as divine bait, luring the devil into snatching a soul over which he had absolutely no right to take: e.g., Gregory of Nyssa (d. 394) used the image of Christ as a fishhook (see *Great Catechism* §24), an image picked up by Maximus the Confessor (d. 662; cf. *Ad Thalassium* §64: "On the Prophet Jonah and the Economy of Salvation"), while St. Augustine, a bit more dramatically perhaps, represented the Cross as a divine mousetrap, while Jesus's blood was the "cheese" which drew the ravenous devil (*Sermon* 130.2).

You have showed us that you are true God and true man.[62] This truth was itself veiled but not purposefully concealed, not made to be hidden, but a truth to come to completion in its own timing.[63] This truth was not meant to deceive anyone but was kept secret so it could become what it was meant to become. And what is meant by "secret" is only that it was not made known to everyone (cf. Mt 13:10–12).

While the truth does not manifest itself to everyone, neither does it conceal itself from anyone. Therefore, Lord, You did what You did not to deceive anyone or to intentionally mislead anyone, but to

---

[62] Following the language of the oldest Creeds and Church councils, especially the Council of Chalcedon in 451, explaining how one divine person can be both fully divine as well as fully human, teaching us that humanity was made for perfect blessedness (as Jesus and Mary both live out) and that while sin, death, and decay may be "normal" after the fall, they are not "natural" in that God never intended such corruption for those made in his image and likeness.

[63] Notice how courteously the fullness of the Godhead is revealed in Scripture: a firm teaching of Monotheism to the Jewish people throughout centuries of the Old Testament drama, then the Son quietly enters the world and then very slowly allows others to know him as "I am," the Son of God, and then after His teaching and miracles and resurrection from the dead, appears the fullness of the Holy Spirit introduced to the world at Pentecost.

do what had to be done, always remaining truthful in all things. And for this reason, those who had deceived themselves while standing in Your truth are really complaining about their own duplicity and not about You.

Questions for Prayerful Reflection

- Throughout this meditation, Anselm relies on the great Christian paradox—namely, God saves the world by first becoming an unborn child, by becoming weak, by dying a criminal's death: "Oh, what hidden strength: by hanging from a Cross a man can lift the weight of unending death from the human race; a man nailed to a tree can loosen the bonds of eternal death which ensnare this world." How might this inversion of what you consider "strong" and "effective" change how you pray and how you understand your Christian discipleship?
- One of the themes of this meditation was tricking the enemy of our human nature.

How does the devil entice you still? What does he use to lead you into sin—fear, the unknown, being easily offended, or easily aroused for lower goods? Ask the Holy Spirit to help you understand the enemy's tactics and for the wisdom and desire to combat these with the Holy Spirit's own power.

- One of the earlier prayers was to Jesus on the Cross. Take some time now at the conclusion of Anselm's meditations to gaze once again on a crucifix and simply be with Jesus faithfully under the Cross. Here you will be with Mother Mary, Mary Magdalene, and St. John. Perhaps one of their prayers will come back to you, but simply be with what you feel as you see Jesus pour out all He has for you and for the whole world.